PHILIP CALLOW

Philip Callow was born in Birmingham and grew up in Coventry. At 15 he went into a factory as an apprentice toolmaker, then was a night telephonist, clerk, teacher, finally a full-time writer after receiving one of the first Arts Council bursaries. Writer in residence at Sheffield Polytechnic for six years from 1980, he has tutored many Arvon Foundation courses in Devon and Yorkshire. As well as novels, he has published ten collections of poetry and five biographies. He has recently completed a *Life* of R. L. Stevenson.

'Callow has a voice which is very much his own; he shows not just intense nervous energy but what seems to be painful nerve ends, an openness to feeling, to suffering and joy at simple, almost primitive levels. What moves him moves the reader. The slant of the world seems his; he has a hold on nature, on the root of feeling.'

Isabel Quigley, *Financial Times.*

Testimonies
New and Selected Poems

Testimonies
New and Selected Poems

PHILIP CALLOW

Shoestring Press

To the memory of my mother,
Beatrice May Callow

Typeset by The Midlands Book Typesetting Company, Loughborough (01509 210920)
Printed by Quorn Selective Repro Loughborough (01509 213456)

Published by Shoestring Press
19 Devonshire Avenue, Beeston, Nottingham, NG9 1BS
Telephone: (0115) 925 1827

First published 2000
ISBN: 1 899549 44 7

Shoestring Press gratefully acknowledges financial assistance from
East Midlands Arts

Contents

FOREWORD

It is over forty years since I first came across Philip Callow's work. In 1956 Cape had published *The Hosanna Man*, and I read it soon afterwards. It's a fascinating book, describing how a young man had come to Nottingham, my home city, to meet a woman-artist he had fallen in love with, and to further his own ambition as a painter. In Hyson Green he makes the acquaintance of a small group of working-class men who read, paint and argue themselves towards the higher life. One passage I remember quite clearly. The hero had been out one evening to visit the leader of this group, the Hosanna Man, and had left his house after what seemed many hours of excited exchange of ideas and had walked back to his digs on a winter's night. He passed a clock, and found it was only eight-thirty.

> "A few moments later I had a moment of perfect lucidity, a wave of tremendous power and energy sweeping through me ... and I felt the inevitable beauty of everything on earth."

Callow perfectly expresses this epiphany. A little later, calling in for a cup of coffee, he sees a poor, elderly man in glasses standing at the counter of the snack-bar, servile, an underdog, never questioning his fate. Suddenly we hear the authentic Callow note.

> "I tried to picture him as a baby, as one who had a mother."

The language seems straightforward, but the apparent simplicity exactly conveys the writer's vision. When I came to read *Turning Point* (1964), his first volume of verse, I found again this opening of a reader's eyes to ordinary events, making us see them precisely as the poet sees them. Two long-distance lorry-drivers have fallen asleep in the cab of their parked vehicle, and lean towards each other. The poet knows that this is not an important matter, that he'll probably never see these men again, but the painting of the picture, the tone of the chosen words so well-matched, ensures that this simple incident takes on the importance of a Chardin still-life, where the objects are nothing much in themselves, but in the hands of a master become a work of art.

His pieces on family life, relationships with other people have this same clarity, immediacy and yet timelessness,

> 'poems that ooze gently like smoke
> without pressure or encouragement
> arrive through those hands squeezing together.'

Callow's words affect the reader at once in these short poems, but without ostentation. If one must look for an adjective to describe his vocabulary, I'd choose 'perspicuous' – lucid – the term Aristotle's translators use when he is writing in *The Poetics* about the language of tragedy. Not that Callow is afraid to chance his arm now and again with more exotic metaphor and even rhyme:

'At night the constellations sang
There in that perfect church, and rang
In the cold belfry of the night
Strewing their splintered light, …'

We see him match his lexis to the colours of Van Gogh, about whom he wrote an excellent book, but the forceful simplicity of his method emerges at its best in one or two of the reminiscences of his father where in a few compact lines he compares his feelings as a small child on his father's shoulders at the speedway stadium with those he felt a year or two later when he dug enthusiastically at the allotment to win his father's praise, which he duly received together with the sensible, chilling advice to slow down, and we learn the depth of his feeling. He asks his father, now 'a ghost in the ground', if he's waiting for him, presumably so that the pair of them could set matters nearer to rights, as he would himself, given a second chance. He had feared, we learn elsewhere, his father's gaze, 'stiff with a winter that would thaw/rarely', but now he knows better.

Each poem widens our view, even as it concentrates it. We join the sick D.H. Lawrence, one of Callow's heroes, near the end of his life in Paris, or Callow himself, a young man, his first novel just published, posing in the garden for his mother to snap him for posterity, or later in life staring down at the school photograph of his class, All Saints Infants I, annotated by his mother, 'second row on the right'. Each poem compels us to consider ourselves as well as the ostensible subject-matter. Look hard, say his words, and we cannot deny them. Such directness is rare with writers because it is so difficult to bring off; try it, and see how easy it is to topple into banality. Callow succeeds so that our every-day world changes. Like Elisha's young man in Dothan our eyes are opened, and though it is certain we shall not be granted the vision of the 'mountain full of horses and chariots of fire' round about the prophet, we shall never see either the humdrum or the unexpected happenings of ordinary life in the same way again.

STANLEY MIDDLETON

from TURNING POINT (1964)

REVOLVING

What nudges me now more than the sun?
Oh dancing, dancing, and I can't dance!
And those gold windows that give hot flashes
At a certain hour –
Sky through the gullet in windowfuls
Rushing huge and blue.

In the restaurant it's a wheel of smiles,
Pakistanis around noon
Moving hardly a ripple.
Their watery friendships touch us all over.
The warm, boneless, male-cancelling handshake!

Then a man at the next table
So clogged with history he is paralysed,
Full of Berlioz, banknotes,
Waving goodbye, his arm sluggish with Raphael.

LONG-DISTANCE LORRY

Red truck slumbering in the alley
at midday, tucked out of sight;
a wintry sun just missing the tin roof.
The driver and his mate fast asleep,
keeled over sideways, both of them,
as if sleep had hit them from one side.
Strangers. I go by surprised,
staring at them through the windscreen.
Unknowns. I go by unknown,
lingering, nobody in sight.
One is yellow about the face,
the other needs a shave.
Babes in the cab. Secrets
and journeys on their eyelids,
their faces bathed with tiredness.
I shall never see them again.

HUNGER

The goaty old man hobbles out
Trembling in the cold

With his eyes congealed,
Scratching his crotch.
Cold! he croaks, Cold! Cold!

Birds tame with hunger,
Birds fighting mad,
Bossless companions of the road.

Half the world's children, UNICEF –
The Korean girl recites:
'When I see the calf getting its dinner

I think of mamma too.'
Still, poems of joy are possible,

My child at the window
Now bread's out
Watching the mad squabbling racket.

Things made of fear and feather,
Bits of bone twitching,

Things made of this age:
She with it –

Her body's sweet pierce of jazz
Agitates the earth.

GENTLE ART

There is never much doubt;
if you aren't at home I find a note
written neatly in italic script.
Nothing visible today, so
I jab the bell and rush in
from the street, smelling of the cold.
Your voice overflowing with friendship
greets me halfway up the stairs.
Poems that ooze gently like smoke
without pressure or encouragement
arrive through those hands squeezing together.
Gentleness is your gift.
You give it over and over,
or in moments of unbelief
dress it in a rustic character
which you invent easily, clowning
for yourself as well as others.
Even then it is gentle art.

ALIVE

It amazes me.
If I am still alive at forty
my amazement will be that much greater.
It amazes me that I am a man,
earning a living in a man's world,
supporting a wife and family,
instead of that youth pedalling for Coventry,
for factories, bombs, searchlights,
or the happy, unhappy child keeping
the deaf old man company on Saturdays.
It is amazing to have grown up
and survived long enough in this world
for my daughter to be now aged ten
with a face of terrifying sweetness.
Having her for a companion on walks,
hearing her laughter, singing, and
as she dances along so unaware
of what a miracle it is, among madmen,
newspapers, just to have these stars.

Just to observe a thrush killed by the cold.
And then suddenly to think something
which could be facile, or a desire for spring:
if we have survived this long, why not longer?

TO AN ACQUAINTANCE GONE TO LONDON

Whenever I met you we were laughing
And I suppose that was no bad thing,
Though it isn't a mood I'm permanently in
And laughter-talking can be a din
To smother nothing; or it can be malice –
Still, now you've gone with your valise
And here comes your letter from the Smoke,
Telling you're lonely and missing folk:
All in the funny ice-skating style
I remember. But I'm damned if I'll
Reply in kind, because I mean to test
Our silence. I wish you all the best.

BIRTH

Going out with stumbling feet
in that November,
running down the street
in the first cold weather,
past the blank chapel wall
to the sharp corner
before dawn or bird-call
or any colour,
you were out of my thought:
nothing was in my head
but what I had been taught
by that pain on the bed.

Your coming was harsh.
Then your body lay sweet
on the cradle sheet.

FRUIT BUSHES

I go home tomorrow.
Clouds hang over the pines
down there on the corner
where the traffic streams.
It is restless, spring weather.
While the dinner cooks
I stroll out with my mother
along the track to the fields.
In the smell of earth,
the heavy smell of fruit bushes,
I walk beside the small figure,
edging into the huge open space.
We skirt a field half ploughed,
step over a knapsack, a flask,
watching a man grow smaller,
driving away down the furrow.
When we come back that way
from the hazels in the gulley
the man has taken his things
and knocked off for dinner.
The spring rain waits, waits
over the Haselbury field.
The fruit bushes stand apart
in long streets like memories.

SNOW

They had been promising us snow for days,
a severe blizzard, on the way from Portugal
of all places! Finally it arrives,
dumping the stuff down everywhere outside
the windows, silently covering Thursday,
turning the asbestos roof of the stores white,
the railway behind that, the bridge,
streets and roofs and sheds and gardens, scrap iron,
drums of cable, the moors and clay dumps far off
and as much of Plymouth as we can see.
Thrilled, we make out we are disgusted,
making cynical noises about picture postcards,
argue the toss about its permanence,

7

whether it is slackening or getting faster,
if it is a blizzard or something calmer altogether,
anything to go on talking about it
and forget the old blizzard of paper on the desks,
anything to gorge on the huge feast of blossom,
sneaking glances at it all the time like children.

TO GO BACK

Suddenly there's this new hardship:
no water in the cottage. Yet
in spite of the intense cold
the tap in the yard next door
still mysteriously running.
So I buy a red can in the village
holding two gallons and go
backwards and forwards with it,
filling up bottles, the washboiler.
Surprised by the weight of water
each time I peer in
at the primitive kitchen.
Stone floor on the slant, the
beams rough-hewed, oppressive.
No sink and no windows.
Washing slung across, two lines.
I couldn't live like that.
But here I am drawing water
as if from a well, almost used to it.
To go back is no more than a step.

A FROSTY NIGHT

All night the constellations sang
there, in that perfect church, and rang
in the cold belfry of the night,
strewing their splintered light
over the bare sea and the humpbacked fields,
while the hammer of frost, that kills
a flower and leaves a feather
on the gatepost, swung from the weather.

All the lanes grooved round the hillsides
shrank; a brittle skin grew over the puddles;
a sharp wind sawed at the birches,
and the sleeping trunks and branches,
cracking their bark and their frozen flesh,
groaned out of a leafless peace,
and the catkins hung limp in the cruel air
where they had danced the day before.

In the clear morning a salt of frost,
flung down thickly by the moon's ghost,
lay on the roofs and the sloping grass
of the rough hills, sparkling like glass.
And like a warm beast in a shippen
the animal body of the sun
was struggling up, and with stiff knees
heaved itself out of the trees.

SECOND SNOW

Gull-white the quick flesh skims in
overnight the sky spilling secrets
world I never made all decorated
white cyclamens hang on thorn bushes
a dead bus staring at passengers
wires aerials smothered in famished birds
a world of violence and Bhattacharya
snakes sing throbbing like flutes
women dance their bellies fluttering
flowers dance and children
the world flutters the world rotates in a snowflake.

9

from THE REAL LIFE (1965)

NOTTINGHAM CITY

Even now it refuses to be familiar.
The windows stare back, unblinking,
the walls are dirtier than I expected.
More cars flood past,
the dark faces drift and multiply.
I am grappling with the ghosts of this place
and don't see the changes.
I come and go on the train,
always half a stranger.
So much has happened here,
I gorge myself over and over
on the same experiences:
wait on the chair again, virginal,
passionate, on a shaky spike of reticence.
Watch the cafe clock, heart blooming,
burning under my shirt wildly, terrible flower,
near the old man selling Michaelmas daisies,
a safety pin fastening his overcoat.
Waiting for pals outside the station,
big-eyed, forlorn,
a born solitary, hugging tight my misery.
A clock crashes the hour, I am a man,
I dive down a street, utterly blind and sick,
running across the square
in a great howl of loneliness,
palely loving, chewing the bitter cud.
Leaves of soot. Telephones and crucifixion.
The icy fog by the river knows me,
the black river, the saturated trees.
People strange as night, in a hurry like me,
stare back as if I had asked them something.
Not so much hostile as unremembering.

STREET SCENE, NOTTINGHAM

A black boy,
his mouth budding open,
no more than five or six

red knitted sweater showing him off,
stands on the pavement one rush hour:
buses stopping, people pouring out

away up the pavement going home;
still he holds his place,
the flood parting round the small figure

the eyes big, solemn;
either waiting there locked out
for his mother or father

or just standing in the way
for no reason that evening.

THE TRUTH

He sat quietly, smiling that smile.
An extrordinary face, black-eyebrowed,
hair thick and black like an art student's,
faded blue denim shirt
careless around the neck –
that ripely sprouting brown stalk
half throttled by a great tenderness.
Tenderness that made him hoarse.
Soft croaking deep in the throat!
I had to listen hard at first,
astounded by such flowering,
not so much the things said
as the sheer fact of him existing,
radiantly open like that,
walking through this century.
Full of brimming nostalgia, his eyes liquid.
The tenderest flesh grieves with a smile.
I wondered how this flushing angel

ever came on the planet.
Marvellous mistake, mad gift!
Later, the halo of his goodness tarnished,
I saw the usual dull colours of living,
met his new wife and new baby,
heard him behave like me – badly.
It was all bitterly familiar, the truth,
and it made sober friendship possible.

LETTER BEFORE YOU LEAVE

You land here at last
and wait around in my house.
Really you, droll in these foreign parts,
spruce now instead of scruffy,
jumping up to meet me
with eyes fizzing, very nice!
Sweetly keeping quiet, droning,
full of the glamour of cities,
those provincial, glittering hives
where you swarm and work.
A touching warmth about you,
yet you're a touch-me-not!
And like me, you don't laugh.
The smile is enough.
The room runs with light,
you were never more approachable.
Anything might happen,
hearts fly open like doors –
that's your wonderful gift.
And all you do is sit here,
dressed for lecturing more than hitchhiking,
a Burtons coat fluttering cheekily
its lining red as a poppy.
You look tired and pleased,
smiling faintly, pale.
At twenty-two you are more travelled
than I shall be at forty.
You lie down for one night,
curled into journeys, roads,
there is no stopping you.

Morning smokes at the window
and I shake your shoulder.
I am as fresh as your expectations.
That's your secret, there
at the corners of your mouth.

CITY NOMAD

A sharp spokesman for the tensely lolling teenagers,
the thick flood of youth swirling the Trentside city,
you sup your beer, smudged subtly among the locals,
chewing peanuts, your eyes pale like a sailor's
with unwritten visions, and dreaming, dreaming
as we beat along dark streets in a taxi,
your mouth registering a faint flicker, saying
'When I go through country I shut my eyes,'
calling yourself flatly a city nomad.
I meet the ponce in a pub in no-man's land
and his girl whores who drift through your place
without affecting you at all, I'd say –
and neither have I even touched the real you.
You sit passive, as if waiting to be killed or caught
by something terrible or something tender
that haunts up and gathers me like a mirror.

GETTING READY

Twitchy, feverish, am alive
in a sickly way, burning.
That cold pinching my cheeks and fingers
this morning on the way in
sits between my shoulder-blades.
Back from a stew of arguments
on prisons, hospitals, homosexuals
shouting the odds all day
two against three.

       Nobody winning,
everybody still in the nick
despite all our talk,
rotting cosily like us
as we finish up in guffaws.

You can't care without faces.
The ferry floats me back uncaring,
past the bakery: no bread smell,
just the shuffling noise over the water.

I'll stay home tomorrow,
try and write. Have influenza. Shiver.
Voyaging to a beginning,
the hour of birth coming on.
No lies. If there's nothing, say so.

ARRIVAL

Going somewhere always churns me up,
frightening. To be tired and excited,
no snow, waiting on the station
pacing it out, and then the carriages
slide in, mysterious, with their
perfectly upholstered white roofs.
Or all the window glass streaming,
and no rain.

        It's like that.
Wondering what will come. Tensely.
My woollen chest rising, falling,
a clock banging its tin rhythm.
Then the silence that pours and deafens.
I get on the poem.

SEE YOU IN THE MORNING

Every day the railings flutter a signal.
They pass me, then the old man appears,
hugging the curve of the wall, never hurrying,
coming closer and bigger, crossing over,
still a leaf of a man, a quick sparrow
in the brown faded overcoat and slewed cap,
his face scalded with wind giving me a grin,
this laundry worker I always have to meet.

Every day, jeans and high boots and high heels,
here they come together, the same bunch
of cut flowers, faces like stunned petals,
moping by in the cold with no breakfast,
hands dug in pockets holding down their coats,
sleepwalking towards the clothing-factory tables.

If I daydream along, if my body's sightless,
if I walk like them, drinking up the road
like a blind kitten sucking up its milk,
I miss the old man, miss the girls, the railings –
and the day's wrong. I remind myself sharply:
'See you in the morning anyway, same time.'

THE MASTER

The little group in the upstairs room
struggle to unpack their instruments.
There has been some muddle and confusion,
the tenor sax player will be along later,
he didn't realise just who was coming.
The big man sits idly in a corner;
disdainful, back arched like an African king,
playing jazz piano for the natives
of this place, who stand humbly,
not expecting to be noticed even.
Doodling gracefully, flamily the master,
when he plays later with the amateurs
he is really solo, a lean, lion-proud
man stranded there in his own desert
by some curious mistake or accident.
Turning his head with fine distinction,
watching the door sideways for improvement,
for the fans to come, for recognition.
Gleaming with gifts, fragrant, wasted.
Nobody knows how it happened exactly.

TOMORROW IS SUNDAY

Late up
   hearing the milk trolley –
  then my child sings out
    the bed pulling
  her now, adult fashion
    still in at ten
    snug by the radio
pops surging down the stairs.

Cats missing –
   no, a big white one
  saunters through (King Ming!)
    the open door
              hollow-flanked hunter
  straight to the back
   to mouse smells under the sink
  tantalising his pink nose
ears ready, sitting sharp with sounds.

Water drums on the skylight
  blackens the street
  sizzles in the kettle
   the tap squeaks
  a woman in the kitchen
    warm, doped, unwilling
           and waking slowly
  inside her dressing gown
writes me a shopping list

And the house alive, coffee-scented
  grows with the day
  liking Saturday night and everybody

a card on the mantelpiece announcing
  jazz, Joe Harriot!

Shopping in the rain dreaming
  my head down composes letters
  asking for cheese new bread brussels
   I remember a flower
   a pressed gentian from Japan

delivered airmail –
how one book a thin one
discharges more
than a man's whole output sometimes –
forget the time don't run
tomorrow is Sunday.

BIRTHDAY

Leaf out of my life,
you're still unbound.
A smile on a twig
that quivers, that gives shocks –
twisting in the sheath
of a prison-grey school skirt.
Thin, crazy white wind.
A green spring
seething up the stalk
of your eleven Novembers,
my sticky bud, French flower.
Free seed of long ago,
I'm your jailor now.

GIRL

Take another look, closer
at those eyes

hooded with despair
like a dull bruise.

Whole years of life
spent solitary

and a great luxury
of the mouth

the way it relaxes
miserably.

YOUNG LIFE

The day begins,
before dawn because it's winter now.
Heaving out of bed
when the alarm crashes,
feeling for clothes in the dark –
then the plunge downstairs,
missing cats, making a grab
for the light switch ...
                    then a pause.
Still more dead than alive
I tune in to the weather
while the kettle stirs.
Farm prices, silence, the over-warm
'Good morning!'
as I duck under the tap,
splashing sleep out of eye corners,
and already the hand's ready
for tying ties and shoelaces.
Pick up a book, just to flick over
and miss the weather,
scoop in cereals with one hand
the other tipping a teapot.
Leap around
until the charge upstairs
to put the clock down in the dark,
pull your eiderdown straight,
whisper goodbye, no it's not raining
and out I go,
thinking suddenly of young life
high overhead there, still silenced,
waiting like the future,
her arms thin, every day a worry
of teachers, timetables,
bursting through the mould
gaily, clean as a crocus,
growing even in her sleep.

MASTER AND MAN

What a tale that one of Tolstoy's —
            the fat furry merchant floundering
away in a panic, terrified
            suddenly arriving back again
by accident.
                        His great joy
                  at finding the other man
the old freezing peasant abandoned
            flopping down on top to save him
the peasant thawing slowly, half dead
                  slowly coming alive
                              then squirming out
from under the dead man at last
                              brothers.

WORDS FOR A PAINTING
(to A.H.)

She looks proliferous, your earth-mother.
She grows like a plant!
Lifesize, which means gigantic
in our tiny passage,
rearing against the wall
with great hips like mountains,
thighs full of rubble and stones,
earth-coloured, struggling massively
out towards the street.
Will she keep spreading, Adrian?
She's geological, boulders
for knees and elbows.
In that timeless sleep
she could give birth to anything!
Wheat, cement, industry,
it could all come marching
from her groin. And worse.
She's dangerous. I keep looking.
At night I lie thinking adulterously
about her, buried under me
black as a miner

at the bottom of the stairs,
secret colossus of Millbrook,
rumbling beneath the boards
with the mice and ghosts.

SURPRISE

Lovely lady, I
Did not expect
To be asked
Into your house.
Oh your rooms
Are delightful,
The pictures and books
Of great charm and interest,
And I can speak
With pleasure
Of the softness
Of a rug,
Though its pattern
Escapes me.
Lovely lady, I
Did not expect
More than a kiss.

SATURDAY

Filling the sky they come,
the slow bushes of foam.
Brown water goes bouncing
down the steep fields, gathering
itself into brook sound
before plunging underground.

Six streets knotted together
keep the families tied here.
Spreading their mud and din
the farm tractors drive in;
children, idiots, old men

watch the hurrying women.
The hills in their old age
stoop over the village.

Nobody watches cloud-cattle
in that Saturday rattle.

THE CONDEMNED MAN REJOICES

The April lanes try to incite us
with the chains of their hedges.
The green goes mad. Foams, fizzes.
The sky is pearly and astonished:
a pure Paris grey, managing skirts of clouds.
Nothing surprises us but Genet,
locked in his pen for a long stretch,
the blanket foul with knowledge –
a surge of blossom in his thief's mouth.

His fantasy is gigantic. It rams the door.
The cell bursts, flowery as an idyll.
He masturbates, his desire leaps like a fish,
sprays us with light like a fountain.
He catches farts in his cupped hands,
offering us bouquets through the bars
and seeing a parade of law books –
holes and eyes and slits –
all on legs scissoring past madly.
We peer out of our slits, terrified, frozen.
The condemned man terribly rejoices.

from BARE WIRES (1972)

DANCING BY THE RIVER

I'm afraid of time stopping
before I've mastered the rhythm.
Life opens in a dream
of slow rivers and your mother
always there in the warm kitchen.
Everything needs slowing up.
The Marx brothers are on TV,
Corporation busmen have come out
but the cars gave lifts
as they did in the war.
A picture postcard floats in
from the summit of Snowdon.
In three weeks I'll be cramming
through college –
and what I should be learning
is how to dance. Slowly.
Dancing by the river
and to hell with reality.
In the dream, and young,
majesty on the fields
and the direct message to the heart
from lips and eyes –
then I could do it.

NOTHING SPECIAL

Dropping in by chance,
passing through the empty afternoon,
not surprised to find you gone;

your lover drunk with sleep,
still in bed after a late party,
propping himself up to greet me

in the big communal room
where the life drifts and ebbs,
young men and women meaning

nothing special to each other,
who are strangers to me.
I sit watching and listening,

thinking how good to be young
when you can stay here or go
and no questions asked;

nothing matters, the world
can lie in ruins outside the windows.
Let it go, while a girl is making tea.

TENEMENTS

It could be tenements in Naples –
except for the weather.
And all that iron.
Bars rising, crossing,
iron landings, iron ladders,
a hard grid facing the sea,
a cage for living in.
It could be Alcatraz
except for the washing,
which decorates it all over
every day
from top to bottom.
The whole structure flaps like a flag.

QUESTIONS

She casts a simple question,
lazily, combing her damp
mermaid hair.
And as he plunges in,
too deep,
talking with such vehemence,
agonising,
opening his mouth soundlessly
between thoughts
like a fish on the beach
        she marvels
at her washed hair,
the auburn tints
and the darkness lost down the sink,
wondering vaguely
why nothing is ever simple for him.

GIRL IN A ROOM

A girl of fourteen
in a room
with two men:
the men looking and not looking,
the girl shy and not shy,
suddenly years older
in this forcing house
of male awareness;
the men hovering wryly
between youth and fatherhood.
One jokes,
drags down his sweater
for a mini-skirt,
skylarks;
the other stares out
thoughtfully
through his bifocals

        while the girl
as if hiding in her hair
seems to be considering
both these solutions.

PRINT

No, not a man
because you said,
'Here's Auntie Pearl.'
The sculptured profile
divides the print,
the opaque disc of her specs
fixed over the grained nose
bored out from underneath,
a black tunnel –

the chin leathery,
losing its tired lines
in a scrabble of grey fusewire
above the goitre

A bludgeoned, Black Country face,
ashy as a wasteground,
which the smile quietly contradicts.

EASTER

The wind sharp over the blue water.
And the grass so dry
we can take the short cut over the marshy field
to the village that sits tight against the wood.

Up and down the huge thighs of hills,
glancing between tree-legs at the city
across the river, glassy and grey-white,
in a ferment with its families,

veins of streets fluid with traffic,
people shimmering in and out
of markets, men on scaffolds, girls
stippled with light drifting from the hollows
of factories.

The pussy willow with its aluminium quiver.
And down by the deserted quarry
the sloe blossom out, the wild cherry.
All young, trembling in a passion

like the new milk, the first wet flower,
and all together, sick with the same desire.
Even the old man near death, staring out
of the cottage, his elbows quiet on the table.

STRAIGHT OUT

Straight out is a sunlit way of saying
What you really mean,
The world being what it is:
I mean the problem of burning clean.

Silence is a fine way of betraying
The stars men hang on trees.
Answers can be dangerous:
Saying nothing is bound to please.

Spring is a bloody time for doubting
The sweet juice of childhood,
Fingering the leaves of paradise
On our way through the wood.

CAT AND HOUSE

We need space.
The great luxury, deep hunger.
I plunge into the city to hunt for space;
meet the bank manager who blinks,
the estate agent with his switched-on smile.
I couldn't be greener.
The solicitor guides me
as if I'm blind, then waits for my instructions.
On the flat roof I feel stupid,
an actor facing an audience of chimney pots.
I drown in light.

Then I see the sea, the heave of headland,
half the city's choppy grey water
sliced up in streets – the surveyor
flapping his hands, angelic, fatherly,
asking me suddenly up there in space
what I do for a living.
I'm struck dumb.
Staring back pop-eyed I look over his shoulder
at fat clouds, bulging with life and no answers.

Head down I make for the bus,
blinded by property and the fear of it.
The young cat watches me,
Buddha-like in the wild grass of the wasteground.
Young enough to be nearly fearless,
coal black with a white bib,
only its shoulders visible,
housed in grass and stationary as a stone.

It wasn't watching until I watched.
Next time it was there again.
How could it sit so still and look so quick?
I saw it once more, symbolic,
like a sign saying: *there's this!*
I was going in to sign the contract.

OLD WOMAN SINGING HYMNS

Everywhere you look, the old.
Mulish, vague, hanging their heads,
blowing and ashy-eyed,
croaking round in circles,
falling over in slow motion.
An old man in green checked wool,
face bloody as a sunset,
fingers so stained
you'd think he smoked tobacco direct from his hand.

So many old,
you feel they're all here
in the far west, the south,
like stones sunk to the bottom.
Old woman singing hymns under her breath.
Some so old they can't remember who they are.
The traffic stamps round them
in a war dance. They wait helpless,
like thrown-away clothes.
Shake them and their skin
would shower a rain of dry needles
like the undersides of gorse bushes.

Old age, that sordid monkey!
I am getting ready for mine.
Come closer
any way you like.
I can shuffle and sing,
I'm a drop-out already.
Hear me spit and talk to myself,
listen to my idiot humming.
I feel a kinship with useless people
shuffling round without guilt.
There are many of us, many.

THREE WAYS OF CRYING

She used to cry
I want an orange, orange!
We played acrobats
where I lay spreadeagled
on the bed in the top room,
legs doubled like a grasshopper
and my feet a quaky platform
for my excited insect of a girl,
wriggling and squealing in mid-air,
who kept laughing, crying ...
And such abandonment
as we collapsed sideways
and she cried *Again!*

I was thinking of the time,
left with her grandmother,
she opened her mouth awfully
like a fish,
blindly hiding her face.
Blind with pain and loss
I went away and was haunted
by that sudden baby spasm.
She was quite old, thirteen,
already skinny and tough.

Now she's older, beautiful,
tall as her mother
and she's outgrown so much,
so soon,
that her backbone's haughty with it.
She combs and combs her hair
to eliminate all childishness,
fringes her eyes with black
and now she's wicked enough
for the worst of this world.
Dreams play in her blood
and her mouth drains,
the curved bone of her nose
traces her young girl's contempt.

O haughty daughter,
ashamed of your birthday suit,
brooding over secrets, problems –
now you make us knock.
Now you cry in private
behind the door.

ENCOUNTER

Nothing in common
except some days and years
stuck in the same office

they meet on the pavement
outside the Ladies',
the older man's bald head

afloat in sunlight,
bobbing up and down
as he talks on

against the raw cliff
of the new college –
chafed at the base

by a river of traffic.
The river slides and screeches,
making them wince

the older man feels sick
so he's going home.
His friend stands exhausted

the weather lovely,
the wife bustling out
into the light, blinking:

nothing in common
except the sun touching lightly
an encroaching weariness.

ANOTHER COUNTRY

Under the sweating arch of the bridge,
before we even see them
we can hear yells
from their playground.
And we know it's theirs
as we move in closer
on our huge legs, two Gullivers.

Swings are rooted
behind the council houses,
green stilts in a patch of tarmac
alongside the railway bank.
The shrieks, clashing chains
die down
for us to enter the arena.

One girl, about six,
has a face like an Eskimo.
Shy in front of the camera
she shuts her eyes,
thinking we can't see her.
Now she's a dead bird.
A boy dances on the curve
of a concrete pipe
while his brother stands tiptoe
to peer through a brick porthole.

Grinning and waving we walk off,
promising pictures all round.
Even acting they're more natural than us.

THE VILLAGE

The Pakistanis who work for him
he calls boys.
They all come from
the same village:
and because their English is poor
they look to him,
more an uncle than a boss,
more a guardian than either.

The restaurant is their village.
When you visit it
they flash a smile
across the fence of language.
In the dappled light of the counter
they are voluble, rapid, really themselves,
waiting for you to go.
The guardian watches.
He arrives home after midnight
and rises late, even
later now because he is married
to a woman he calls
Princess of the Sleeping Kingdom.

from NEW YORK INSOMNIA (1976)

FLYING

Into it, hardly believing
It would be there
Any more than Columbus —

Then stamping on the ground
Astounded
Repeating over and over
The word America

Speechless before
Those sights
Smells
The unbelievable dereliction
Crash of packed life
Splintering through streets
Acre upon acre of ratty slums —

Hallways like visions of hell —

Going round for six weeks
Marvelling
Rubbed raw all over
Writing it on postcards
Drunk on rivers of faces

Then flying back
Into the waiting cotton-wool kindnesses
The pleases and thank yous
Cooing in his ears

Safe in the dream of disbelief.

MANHATTAN

Steaming, hung up in strips
At the edge of the sea –
That maze, web and rock,
Scaffolds of concrete fuming in the distance,
Miracles of glass misting over
As a backdrop for shattered tenements,
Block after stinking block

Then at night,
Balanced on the water –

Beautiful jewels

An Atlantis rising
To seduce you with electricity.

Next day,
Ugly boxer –

It slams you with streets
Bolted together with fire escapes.

What crazy men,
Lurching out of the stone and iron,
Scalded with liquor,
Wearing clown-trousers,
Their terrible faces in rags,
Stumble-bums of all ages, races.

Hands cringing out
They halt there
At the wire of your fear.

Every summer
The whole city burns
In the fork of its rivers.

FROM A ROOF GARDEN

He could see
Through chinks in the fence
A thin young black
Strutting purposeful and foreshortened
To the liquor store,
And two ferocious whores,
Visored like vultures,
Perching on the next corner.
Ahead, the brown block
Of Cooper Union,
Gateway to the Bowery

Yellow cabs
Scudding to beat the lights

Suddenly
The Chrysler Building
Jabs its bright finger
Out of the smog
And suddenly
A man with a bottle
And a shaved head
Wiggles his hips crazily
Along the Avenue,
Dances on the gridiron,
Grabs at steam,
Tears off his cap,
Tramples it underfoot
And howls at the sky like a wolf.

ARTIST

On Brooklyn Bridge, ninety degrees of heat
He kept walking

And took pictures from all angles
Of that fabled skyline

The sun banging down
On hawsers, girders, trestles

Oily water, the lids of cars
The smog so bad it was like using a filter.

People admire his pictures
And those stone towers looming ghostly

The bald old derelict
Slumped sideways on the bench

Dead, drunk, or ill
His dreams tangled in that enormous harp.

One missing picture, not so pretty
Is of the artist

Getting the subject in his viewfinder
And then walking on oblivious.

THERE HE IS

In what they call a railroad flat –
A line of rooms shunting along
One behind the other,
Kids under the windows outside
Splitting the great blocks of heat
With firecrackers

As he limps about,
This unknown poet from Alabama,
His long-legged dancer wife
Pouring fresh wine on the rocks.

46

Smouldering in a chair
He seems clenched around something
Which could be hate, or genius, or merely
Anger and light crackling together,
And then something else
Hooding over bland as a cat
As he says smiling,
'America is a state of mind,'

In one stroke
Halting it all for one second

So that the kaleidoscopic city hangs there
With its million bits
Not shaking any more,
Just falling to the ground everywhere
                                        quiet.

BIOGRAPHICAL NOTE

Growing up one day in fear and trembling
He had a dream of love
Like a fresh flower opening
Just for him

Kisses raining on the heart,
The whole of life a beautiful
feast of blossom.

He woke up in tears of grief
For some reason.
He was most hurt
When they got him in a corner later
And told him a dirty story.

Afterwards
His cunning body spawned hate
In howling cities.

TWO PICTURES IN A FRAME

1.
Duke Street.
The square with a statue.
Town hall big as a cliff,
people in a thick traffic,
tangled up and pulsing
one Saturday.

Head down, hunting for loaves,
diving through side streets –
I could have missed them.

There they were –
he in the snakeskin jacket,
pale-haired, the face bloodless,
his young negress, black
as he was white

splashing her quick scarlet
on the granite town.

2.
A nail in rotten wood.
Shack on a cliff.
Nailheads weeping rust,
the tin roof spongy in places,
the room for sleeping in
no more than a cupboard

its board wall
pricked at night
by a swinging lighthouse beam
far out.

And then the mornings.
Chinese mist.
A slate sea. A world holding
its breath –

I sniff at the coconut-scented gorse.

48

AFTER SEEING THE FILM *SOLARIS*

Out with heartache
Under a night sky
To webbed trees
Shaking before the birth hour
Of a huge slow star
Delicately cracking open the dark

Because the grey father has been transfigured
Glimpsed through a window he is baptised
The water steams in warm curtains from the ceiling
Over his head, moustaches, the old skin
                                    of his cheeks

And we are leaving now
The great roar of space-silence lifts us off
The son kneeling below
Sculptured by tools of light

The scene with its figures shrinking
The wooden house, the small island world
The curved water that shrivels
As we hurl back on soundless fires
The shrunk sea bursting far below
on tiny shores

Pretty chaplets of foam turning to wrinkles
Cloud mist
The time tolling
                    in vast watering arcs
As if a new god is breathing.

PICASSO'S OLD AGE

The head moves, the jaw sideways-snapping

A squat shape
Fleeing blackly with oar-limbs by the edge
    of the sea
Under the dreadful sky-flap and the beach
    with footprints

A sea scrapes at bones and delivers figures

The old man of straw with insect eyes
Glowing purple at evening
Flees into vast labours, he attacks with bare hands
    a whole ocean
Of the hairy genitals of women

Tearing at them in brothels
In cold rages in a slobbering
They erect in hundreds and surround him
He makes haste
His keys hung on string
Fruit all over his body in large bunches
Wear through his clothes in no time
And there is no sewing done

A big key –
For there is always a door somewhere –
Thrust out for trying.

TO COME LOOKING

I have a demon snarling in the pit of me,
the lies snivel out of my hair,
when I walk my feet kick out like murderers,
I stand against a wall, I rotate flailing
and go down and begin the slow crawl
up the slope to the face gravely averted
and the word withheld

for the lack in me to be made good,
for the smile to come looking, to be given.
Out of the black animal sneaks a hand,
into the cool well falls a peach stone.

PICTURE BY SYDNEY NOLAN

Call it a trance in shades of green
Where I go swimming daily.

It has a title,
Baptism.

A huge baby glowing on its side
On a bed of watery air

Below a tree-thing
Guttering like a candle

Its few fronds blowing sideways
Flamily

Away from that event.
In the treetop

A couple livid with the whiteness
Of a certain love

Lie puny,
Cuddled in ecastasy-fright,

Male and female rudiments
Dwarfed by the great moon child.

51

CAT

Just there,
Passionately faithless,
Swaying your pelt
You make shadow in the doorway
As if to tantalise me

But you're without desire or contour,
Wavering superbly, black smoke.
I'm a puzzle, a judder of vibrations
Up your sniffing monkey nose,
And then the charge ripples hot blood
In your twitchy snake tail.

The sparks fly from your fur invisibly.
Circling, approaching sideways
You show the glowing bulge of green beads
As your toes know the rough matting
Finely, like a dark dancer.

Fierce with appraisal you run
The river of your black body closer,
Haunches coiled for the leap.
The landing, soft as the dew wetting,
Prises open a wild flower mouth
To unlock rank breath, the meat.

PAINTING BY MIRO

Slab of inky black. And a thin sky
Gaily dribbling electricity.

Which is perhaps why
The hacked sun and the moon
Confront each other, wounded

There in the same corner, wobbling
And grinning wickedly
From ear to ear

A red field putting out its delicate
Paper flags of flowers
For the yellow horned woman

Who gnashes breasts and eyes,
Goading the vivisector
To do his worst.

BORN UNBORN

The earth-body in flight,
Barrelling on with a roar of tides
While an amazed eye watches –
Sunrises and midnights in a steady monotony

Dying and blossoming nonstop –
Lives, birds and plants, diseases
Cobwebby alleys
All slithering in unison along grooves
                                        down spirals
Like a dog blundering after its bitch,
Lapping and eager

Never rests –

Neither the fire nor the water,
Slavering round full tilt
A vast body fired and then forgotten

   It breaks loose
             it guzzles up the space
Bathing in lustres
Whale-gentle among starry plankton
Gobbling at the void
           circling and dancing
In a huge untutored rhythm
A gross beast steered blind for nowhere
It goes grazing
On lost fields of light

Nobody falling off or dizzy, nothing,
Not a single pebble
Tree-hairs and oceanic eyeballs intact,
Lakes winking in the pelt
The pricked stars of fires visible
Disasters clinging to it all over
Raging boils of cities, cracked scabs

Singing and swooping round always
In a great song of numbers
In the shuffle and serve of its seasons
Crackling alive
All graves
With a pale sea-belly
Through the blue

Delicate as a fern unrolling in the hedge bottom.

from CAVE LIGHT (1981)

BRENTOR

The moors turn brown, rusting out.
High over the village they wait for winter,
wearing heather like a disguise.

Lying down wide open
their enormous bodies dominate me,
lodged with pebbles and rocks,
body fluids oozing
into bogs from secret places.

They are lying in wait. Touching.
They are fecund.
If I walked into them far enough
they would suck me in like sensual parts,
swallow me up like a lover.

Everywhere I look, sea-swelling,
burning with colour their breast-berries,
overwhelming me their thighs' desire,
opening and closing, sighing,
streaming their hair.

Great lonely bodies
full of hollows
for our small lonelinesses.

NOONTIDE

The young October sun rolling and dog-hot
The air shining like bright glass,
The day seeming to rest and then break
Like a shallow wave on a long white beach,
Arresting slowly and with the movement still in it

The spider taut on his web engineered marvellously
From the tips of cotoneaster twigs,
Delicate as breath, stronger than steel bars,
He has made it so that a gale could blow through,
He can lower himself and then climb by
Winding the thread back into his plump belly,

He has been constructed in two halves,
The black seam showing thick as a charcoal line,

On his humped back the terrific markings
Of the tiger and snake combined.
He scuttles off at a touch and acts dead
In the corner, like the cat
On warm earth all sluttish
That feeds its white fur to the sun,
The air quietly rolling a ball of heat forward

Full of a morning's sounds among old trees,
The deep bins greedy for fruit, a child
Repeating 'grand day' over and over
And the mother still picking,
The day running in to rest for a moment
With its work before turning, before
The long afternoon moves slowly
Its warm slack length out of the sun.

FOAL

Tenderly on stilts
he leaves the mare and approaches,
he keeps a long head ducking
to the buckets of air,
the wandering path in the grass
visible only to him,
his muzzle softest leather
on the cold iron of the gate.
He wears flies for eyelashes,
he pokes out a loose flap of rubber
in a shock of tombstone teeth
yellow and gummy like a camel's.
There is a thin black prick
darting out in an angle of excitement
like an exclamation mark.

58

A POCKETFUL OF APPLE LEAVES

A wet mist rolling away to the road
And the letter scrawled in a hurry
The fruit foreman hanging dull in the aisles
As a worried grandmother falls spreadeagled
The apples smothered in dews and earwigs
Ladders pitched and pointing to heaven
With a purgatory of labour under crooked arms
A wooden chamber rumbling like a huge stomach
The morning harvest gathered and paid for
A leather knee-length coat sold to a man
Who comes up grinning all over his bald head
The surprise visit of a bald almond baby
Wobbling and roaming her eyes everywhere in
A bliss and sluice of unknowing
After you hear the rustle in a denim shirt
Of a pocketful of apple leaves
Gathered by your pocket under eyes of apples.

COBWEB GATES, FOG BODIES

Web-lines slung across the dim yard
one night
Like fairy spittle

The feathery-quiet feel
Of unimaginably discreet kisses

Cobweb gates, fog bodies
Whispering and still

Big as fields

A million filigree entrances
Disguised as fly traps

Wetness. Softness.
Diffuse, dreamy flesh,
The way it touches and lets go,
No obligations, it means nothing –

A pure joy; the first wet wonderland.

MICHAELMAS DAISIES

Outside the window
A soft explosion of mauve stars.
The massed gleaming of pollen-heavy, dark
    yellow eyes!
Dozens of green pointed tongues
Go softly licking. The very air spills
Them out of its full womb.

The amber light's kind rinsing water.

Even the stones of the wall,
Softened to look like suede, are ineffably
    drenched,
Settling down on themselves with the airiness
    of birds, of a cloud,
Feathered with soft sun.

The autumn sky at night gives birth
Without uttering a sound. Out rolls the biggest
    moon-child of all
To astonish us

And then hangs there, nearly touching
    the ground,
Solid as butter,
Brown as corn.

YELLOW

The lit meadow of the once-great park,
Noble trees here and there,
Decapitated elms standing about
With the presence of lords
Stunned by their fate.
The way the thick yellow light butters
My feet.

Lying down in the spiky cow-field
To be sunstruck, hot-rolled.
The footpath winds up a woman and a dog

And a good afternoon
And I rise for my walk.
The poplars straight ahead make noise
Like a fence of water.
The cool air hits me like spray.

DAFFODIL BUDS

Gathered up rough-snapped
in stiff shudders
on a farm near Ponsanooth
they look cold still,
propped in the tin bucket
leggily for sale —

suffering there on the wet pavement
to the blare of fruit.

The colour of sickness nearly.
Sharp greenish wounds
stained yellow by a too vicious
and stopped Spring.
Numb fingers. Cut to the quick
by a fine knifing wind.

The chill little phalluses
poke at the air feebly,
full of nothing but spite.
Wrap them in papery love-tissue
for the soft carrying off,
the slow melting

in the plank chamber of a sea cottage,
massaged with warm air.

THREE FALMOUTH SCENES

1. Bright as a surprise.
    all cutting edges
    the cold words run out,
    lathe-shavings of a heart
    stiff in its own dryness
    at the sight of me.

    The cracks open like old wounds,
    a black swirl murderously shutting
    bounces my fists on walls.
    The cry rips,
    I can bleed tears,
    kneeling in the doorway
    of a March seizure.

2. A parched and dark
    whispering woman
    coming in under the protection
    of wings of hair
    returns the tiny picture
    of love-bugs
    she has anointed with linseed oil.

3. Laid out below here under trees
    is a damp glimmering tapestry
    of purple and white crocuses
    heavily agape in the thin grass.

FROM THE LETTERS OF RILKE

He is eating figures,
He will die if they force him;
With a backward movement he begs bread,
Drowning in the wash of his regret.
How can he live? He waits, waits –
Up to the knees in a thousand details.
Even the rough light has a dagger;
The yawning parks of big cities
Gobble him up. He begs on
In a surging tide, he sees Roman steps

Built in to the patterns of water,
The stairs thrusting him forward
As he descends shining,
The pages printing themselves
In the very eye of the storm.

THE LOST MOON

The sky a huge bruise
Blowing nearer

I saw trees in the great park like fountains
The sun struck at them, tall
Open gowns of leaves
Twittering like birds like silver water

You have let the dark in
The day is death to you
The world wears itself out
On the edge of some sick hole

Put out the box and a message
For the loaf of bread to jump in

The rain fitful, the rain pouring
Like your lost moon with its fringes

When you touch the table it spills salt –
'Oh,' you cry, 'Oh'.

WINTER KNOWLEDGE

The big bullock saw me, its legs
Stopped, it looked as old as me.
With the fodder hanging and ragged
In wild fringes as it forgot to munch,
Uncomprehending head like an old man
Behind the fence of an asylum.
It was red mud breathing.
I went over cow tracks smothered
By the sift of big-handed leaves,
Frosted and perfect shells that broke
Under my gumboots like potato crisps,
Fine crackings. I could do nothing
Harmful, they were too many, I saw them
Perfect and dead underfoot,
They broke open beautifully. Passing
A wood I peered in, it was dark as
A boneyard, I was inside ventricles
and lungs that had been rotting.
I passed by, hearing
The wood drip from its one mouth
As all the frost melted together.
Then across the stream and beside
The round copse it slunk out, the fox,
Breaking cover it slipped down to drink
While I changed state: I was a post
Wrapped in a duffle coat.
The glass of steel specs caught the light,
It saw me and doubled back, up
The sprinkled salt to the green tablecloth.
My heart shook to the twist of its head
As it glanced over. Entering the lair
Of trees dulled it, the white flare
And the dense drooping brush went out.
I was set going, I had a heap
Of rotting apples to sniff at the top
Of a choked track, the cidery smell
Fetched me. And then a squirrel
Shot loose in swift rippling shudders
As if to demonstrate the grace there is
In things verminous. While these
Ran from me and were painting themselves
The sun poured colour, I was part
Of the frieze, golden and caught.

64

from ICONS (1987)

ONCE

There's this person he once was,
hardly a man,
ill in the midst of fields
and without light,
unable to tell bird from leaf.
His heart's tiny leaps. Beating against
the dry walls of himself.

Who knew something irreversible
had happened, on that past ground
where we take hold and build.
Which haunts us. Where we can't linger.

Except, once or twice, in dreams.
Waking each morning
to the same dread, getting dressed,
his unhappiness in every fold.
His one labour the recollection
of what he'd dreamed.
As if the truth, pinned down,
would redeem all,
and his thirst for love leave off.

He is in a hurry to slip out,
to avert his eyes. Takes to the street,
hugging the burden which comes from
giving and receiving nothing.
Knife-wind, knife-face.
Everywhere dead surfaces that deflect, say no.
Going forward to a room
with one chair, a trestle table, corners,
the window swimming with a view.
A bare plank floor. Echoes of solitude,
of another's terror. Laughter from below.
Running out of there and coming on
the bleak, out-of-season sea.

'That's not it.' A dream
like a hole, full of beautiful pleasure.
He embraced the woman warmly.
Closing her eyes she sighed, smiling,
and began to gyrate.
A child-man, he hung on to her skirts,
floating out like a slow roundabout
in the bliss and grace of this solution.

Speechless, the man at daybreak,
crushed back into his years,
is like the moon. He is all dream flight.

NOON TRAIN

You draw near.
Light years of travelling bring you in
on a gleam of rails. No more delays.
I go forward stiff-legged,
you step down through a door,
a small bag, a new coat,
shyness wearing a smile.

Faltering on the brink. It's ordinary.
My magician's flowers whip out
from behind my back,
five anemones in a caul of tissue,
mauve, white, blood-red,
the eyes blind, thick-wadded.
Moth-bodies that loll in a huddle together
on plump snaky stalks.
I am saying something or other,
our legs walk,
a city we don't recognise, don't hear,
roaring its concrete head off.

Extraordinary woman, you see me!
Your eyes prick, the drug runs in.
Hanging on to your arm I feel dizziness,
I have you now. The influx
takes hold and I stride along at your side,
we cut through as one.

The bus moves, the glass quakes.
I buy two tickets. So our dream has its price
like everything else. Laughing,
we get a little drunk on this
and on each other, affording it.

KNEELING SNOWDROP

When it is still, when its head hangs,
safe among that clump we saw together,
dreaming past in our false spring
and as if soldered to the one smile −

ask what it knows, hacked at by ice-winds,
bludgeoned by frosts. Dawns approach it
with knives, ropes, hammers. So frail,
and yet nothing can kill it!

You could pinch out its trembly
snowflake life
between fingers without any pressure,
with the beak-nip of a sparrow.

A cold merciless as absence rages,
shrieks murder, darts round the corner
at a hunched figure muffled to the eyes
and still suffering.

In a winter of doubt I hang on,
roots lost in a freezing darkness that will
melt again one day like your countenance,
when you are still, when your head hangs.

SERVITUDE

The walls stare back.
I hug the pain of my confinement,
I know pride, my lips
are fitted to a grin.

Your skin was kind, and it touched me,
a foot nudging us
towards a need.

Lying in the womb
of a warm bath, my
life hangs about to be used up.
The servitude is ignoble.
Grinding my teeth
over the old umbilicus.

SMILE

We know when to be happy
and when to wail.
When to sit still
and when to sing.

As if your heart melts.
As if my heart stops.

We have legs in agreement.
Our arms reach for bodies.
Hands are cunning with fingers,
feet laugh with toes.

In your eyes, the answer
to the question in my eyes.
That I dare not ask.
That you dare not acknowledge.

You're acquainted with death
and in you I embrace death,
with fear and with trembling,
with your hand on my head

with a faint smile a smile.

SCHOPENHAUER IN LOVE

The light was ebbing out
until I longed for you in pitch darkness.

At least I am still alive.

Carnality is this thin rain
falling on a man's naked skin.

There's security and warmth now,
and what a burden of ennui.
I can't move for it.

You creep nearer. You have an honest laugh.
Oh and your lips. That word.

If the word love tears my heart to utter,
will survival be worthwhile?
At the cost of this pain,
shall I be free of the struggle
to kill time?

It's too great a step from these ruins.
I sit groaning here, with clear eyes.

You creep nearer.

IN THIS ROOM

A snowfall to bury and lose flowers,
it drowns as it gathers. Even thickening
to a fast gruel, who takes it seriously?
A last tease, prettily
sprinkling petals from the late March sky.
Pale eggy light, newborn, stuns
with surprise the hard wet baskets
of treetops.

In the strewn flat
you've left your nightdress behind,
and a silence that reels about
by the drunk bed. Everything has changed.

The wooden table acts stupid
and remembers nothing.
Looking round, I can see that none
of these objects
belong in a home now.

Beyond the glass, with shy touches,
the feathering snow
assists at an old ritual of dying light.
Time slinks by in this room like a rat.

NO WORD

Can you imagine what I am seeing?
Painting over the clouds, a sickle
like a white question mark above us.
And in all directions, streets running.
Faces everywhere. Voices.
Bodies that can give no answers
cling together.

The wind from the north, swinging its edge,
says nothing, just attacks
the scared underbelly of my hope.
Daffodils in green bud,
spring's fistulas, urgently demand
a word from some warm, kind place
if they are ever to be transfigured.
To rejoice.

Love-lorn, three students
haunt the staircase
where a phone might ring.
My key opens a hall door.
Standing here alone
is not nothing. As if in my skin,
the painful misfortune of a room,
its air trembling. Walls
that have jostled to revive
echoes of you.

COLD FLOWERS

You tell me,
'I've got a housebrick growing
in my chest.'
The train hurtles us over fields.
A sleek death. Cuttings everywhere
studded with primroses. Such a sweet
splashing of the new grass, the soft faces
cruelly fingered, the tiny blades pulsating
in cold gusts.

We sit in luxury. The riches drain from us.
It is over. I bite into an apple
and feed you the last bits of myself.
Doors that slide open untouched,
in this machine nothing stops, and intent
like love on its own processes.

The lit gulch of your station
sucks us to a halt.
I couldn't speak my love.
Now my belly's a slush of nothingness.
When you go, I lose everything.
Unless you go, I can't even hope,
suffocating in this silence
we have grown, and now occupy.

And no turning round. It has been arranged.
Seeking you in vain, what I see
is my own hungry face,

smudged on the glass
and distorted by flaws.
Its black tears won't weep.
Dementedly it stares out. Opens
its creature mouth.

Now the icons with strange forms
will take root in my luggage –
bitter, pain-struck eyes
and your grin's stubborn sun.
Shinings of cold flowers.

ALL

It goes on all the time,
in the street, on a train,
sitting quietly alone,
face to face in the mirror.

How can such a power
trickle in between lips,
wreathing a brow delicately,
invisibly, like moon waves?

I get out of a car
and my journey is still in it.
(The hands steering are no longer mine).
One engine purrs, another shunts,

my skin webbed like a map.
Love possesses all for its own ends.
Tissues wounded beneath the light
knit together again eagerly

for the transmission of messages.
In the streaming lovelessness
of a packed city bazaar, then underground
towards the gleam of cold tracks

connections are being made.
Arteries pump love.
Nothing held dear is ever really smashed.

from SOLILOQUIES OF AN EYE:
A van Gogh Sequence (1990)

CHILL OCTOBER

Ghastly, these shortcomings,
when one wants to work, to paint out
one's guilt, and is afraid of friendship,
the simple spell of an eye,
or of even the consequences
of moving a muscle.
Always the treacherous uncertainty
of the artist. The task's enigma.
'Come closer and you'll be sorry!'
The bitter leper's old cry
is torn from you
and you see him, he walks from you,
a sad shadow
backing fearfully from everyone
with a pounding heart.

SOUL OF GRASS

All the time you go looking for blue.
In the ripe corn.
Between the shrivelled leaves
of a beech hedge.

Who could imagine the coarse linen –
abused by the sun and rain,
fading delicately under cold stars

that the people here weave for themselves
and wear superbly?

Only you, standing still and astonished
with your soul of grass.

DIGGERS IN A TRENCH

I love black, black.
The paper's grey, it's been rained on.
Nobody sees me, I am too ugly.

I stand back and observe,
invisible as the poor.
Noise and mud. Movement.
Noise and mud. Confusion.

My old coat comes into its own.
Will you say I'm lowering myself?

Manners are founded on goodwill,
so I make marks,
the water and gas pipes go in,
I stand in the mud with workmen
and we do our best.

If I could manage it
without disturbing anyone
I'd jump down in that sand trench
for another angle.

One bends, shovels. One turns his back.
The foreman puffs on his pipe.

Grey blotches, a dragging hobnailed line,
broken diagnoals of a life in motion.
Oh, I shall be complained about!
I fit in, I harmonize too well with these men.

It doesn't matter now
about the rip in my jacket.
Nobody notices the freak who draws anywhere,
in all weathers, at all costs.

MEN AND WOMEN MINERS GOING TO WORK

The sun coming up.
They are on their way through snow
towards the pit shaft. In a line.
On ruts. Beside a thorn edge.

Heaps of clinkers loom up –
and then the buildings, dire.

It's true I'm homesick
for the land of pictures.

Remember: these people are white!
They stumble out into daylight
like a mob of chimney sweeps.

A scattering of poor huts
goes along sunk lanes
into the woods, and up the slopes of hills.

You have to search
for these moss-coloured roofs.
At night, maybe a candle
shining through a pane.

Remember: many are sick here. The village stinks,
a dismal labyrinth
of hut alleys.

Men old before their time,
and their women faded,
on their feet wooden clogs,
on their shoulders the dead weight of everything.

Remember: the trees are black with smoke, dying.
Dunghills. Ash tips.
Coal that doesn't burn but only smoulders.

Life exists at the edges,
in the flutter of a bird's wing,
or it goes underground.

Remember: their bodies belong to labour.
And no colour.
White as grubs guttering under black.

While above ground
there is only waiting and silence.

It's true I sleep on a plank now.
It's true the evangelists have lost faith
in me.

Like a bird that's menaced
I plunge dangling with the miners.
But in spirit. I am left to mourn.

Trembling,
I go down inside myself.

FEMALE NUDE STANDING – ANTWERP

The model's ugly. Belly and buttocks jut,
    so you think of power.
Just to look charges up coarse lusts.

A raw servant girl, the face smallpoxed,
    shrimp-coloured in patches.
Two or three months gone, or maybe more.
    A squat, healthy body,
and she stands like a plant, as if her toes
    were roots.

These bodies bear, they suckle,
and because of this they store energy
    and it crackles forth.
Disturbed, you want to paint and to possess
    them, both at once.

Rubens was here, and you see Rembrandt
    everywhere.

Somehow, you expect a tough hide
    when she undresses.

The flesh waits unseen with its surprise,
   its strong shadows.

You find beauty anywhere.
In a single teardrop.

FROM THE DETAILS OF A LIFE

Ordering you to pack and leave,
the landlady testifies,
'They don't like your face.'

Speechless, you avoid her
as the day's motif has avoided you.
Staggering drunk with sun
you make for the stairs,
with the wet junk
you are forever carrying, dropping.
Smearing the walls.
A sad porcupine,
you walk muttering, and you could be
a dog, a bird, lost
somewhere in the hot south.
In whose country are you orphaned?

You're not really here.
Strung up, moving in fits and starts.
Your head burned on the top
to raw meat; eyes sore and red
like a syphilitic's.
As long as there's a hole
you crawl in it: that kind.

Your mouth a fire pit.
Your charred lips. Anyone can see
you're burned up, burnt-out.
You swing from the sun,
hurtle from dawn to nightfall
and then crash into here.

Lodgers feel hellish,
just to look at you.
As if it mattered. As if they lose
when you lose.

THE YELLOW HOUSE

Roulin, the postman,
who had a home and family,
he saw it first.

Hunger! What did you have?
Lonely as a wolf,
what were you after all
but a flogged, never-stopping
painting machine

who dossed down in the coffins
of putrid rooms?

The brass bed. The cracked pitcher.
Always the table or chair
with a rotten leg.
And you can depend on it,
the washbowl's filthy.

How to believe a man
looking like him – like God.
Roulin's great wavy beard,
and such eyes –
telling you how beautiful he was.

In that blinding light.
These Arlesians!
The wind lacerates, then the sun.
It chars the brains till they're all *fou*.

At the town's edge,
mid summer,
seeing it you said
how much?

Fifteen francs a month.
The walls yellow.
And inside, deep silence.
And a cool stillness that descended
like a blessing.
Floors of scrubbed tile, blood-red.

A clean start could begin here.

What a place
to be lonely in.

AUGUSTINE ROULIN WITH BABY

The mewling child in its white gown, white bonnet,
rigid with distress it seems,
held away in a strange impulse
by the mother,
standing in profile with her head bowed,
who splays her fingers
as though denying something,
a finger-speech perhaps of protest,
a denial of closeness
or the fear of it.

Behind them both, the deep yellow mortar
of a pounding sunlight,
nourishing without mercy what it falls on,
urging growth on all things,
doubt as well as faith.

AFTER A PORTRAIT

The Arlésienne stares back,
brazen and yet mournful with her
mere hour of praise. Against
pale lemon,
a grey elongated face.

But why resentful? At being
slashed at, dragged from nothingness,
and in such brutal haste?

A raw Prussian blue,
lurking in the folds of black clothes,
begins something else: the
ferment of lilac, cataracts of dawns.
For all that, wordless

she leans on a green table
and exists,
trapped in an armchair of orange wood.

PAINTING OF FARMS NEAR AUVERS

Ramshackle thatch that gapes in the
        shimmery weather
like an old hat nobody throws away.
A countryside growing farms like crops.
You rinse them through a child's eye,
and you have them touching.

They lean in on each other.

The walls blue, pure spirit.
The earth airborne, heaving up in the
        atmosphere.
And the stick legs stretching down
of three ostrich trees tied to the ground.

No animals

but the fields walk their own hides.

Not a human face. But the bushes
are laughing –

the warm blurting laughter of
                        your heart's submission!

It all joins, copulates,
flows and yearns in contours.
A small universe, yellow as an egg.
Pulsing and still, it waits like a lap.

THE REAPER

Wheat and sky are the same solid gold.
A field enclosed by a wall as long as life,
huts for shelter, the sun
rolling, pressing
its hot belly
along the crags and humps of blue hills.

Finding the reaper – the world's oldest puzzle.
Between the sheaves, in a guise of yellow,
the green glint of his scythe
the one ghostly clue.
At his long task,
the dizzying heat nothing to him,
in the human oven of man's toil
he draws near. He comes close, closer,
his blade hissing a smile.
He is never late. This is a happy death.

ZOUAVE

Here's a boy whose small face on a bull neck
 goes with
his brassy head, his blue uniform – enamel blue
 like a saucepan.
He registers as a series of jolts, vulgar.

He's a beast, a wild cat; his eye leering.
 Against the orange bricks
of a wall, in his reddish cap, near the
 peeling green of a door
he looks loud, savage. You learn something
 in a way.

Is this the portrait of a new face,
 strange to art,
staring out over its domain?

SORCERY IN A FIELD

In a cage of heat,
hungry convict enriched by light,
you mix yellow, you give up the struggle,
entering the strange haven

of your brain's lacuna –
a meek meadow of nothing hurtful,
that is out of sight,
running over with unsought love.

Out of habit you stay upright,
baring teeth like a fox,
beautiful at last through stealth,
in the supple cunning of your approach.

What have you seen? Beyond the glare,
a new simple goddess of the fields
burning, a white flame
begging for shape and colour.

FOUR SELF-PORTRAITS

1
He set to work inventing himself.
Cancelled out, inferior,
he draped success over his shoulders
like cigar smoke.
'Gentlemen, it fits. This will
please my parents.'
Like a man of substance in his fine coat.
signalling with his white shirt collar,
its high wings, its tuft of blue.
And to crown all,
the amazing grey felt hat.

Eyes telling their own story
slid sideways,
looking fearfully back
into his head.
Was the mirror him?
Staring at it, confused –
the bad actor, dressed
and struck dumb
at the thought of uttering his lines.

2
Hating Paris, he turned violent publicly,
a roughneck who used colours,
a coarse-petalled sunflower,
hairy-stemmed, indelicate.
And his face broadened to withstand insults,
wearing peasant blue,
the eyes holes
and behind the mask, ingratitude,
on the clutched palette
the waiting body of Arles.

3

In a roar of flame at one sitting
he ignited,
fiery beard, skin and hair,
nose and eyes laid back
in a blistering redness
from the devil's furnace.
All his friends were consumed
and his mouth twisted.

4

Finally, he was Japanese,
with eyes slanted
and head shaved to the skull,
his throat bare
to fate, to the sharp leaf
of the suicide's razor.
Left out, and nothing to be done,
looking in demented
at the world's wedding party.

Around him, in a soundless song
touching the earthy jacket,
the unimaginable green of paradise.

CRACK OF LIGHT

Stunned by
the nakedness of things seen,
the painter's stare missing nothing,
'ravished, ravished by what I see,'
trees, houses, death, fungus.

Dumbstruck
before women,
the model exposed but not him –

shrunk to a peephole crack,
flesh trembling to be unseen,
peering out through fingers over eyes,
self-blinded nearly
by the core of shame.

Such a pain to be looked at.
A face bandaged with fingers,
blinded by suspicion

and just a crack of light.
Hope squeezing in.

HOMESICK

You, whom I love, shine still.
Though I cannot come
I lie longing
for your troubled skies, nude tombstones

sombre grasses,
the sea of furrows
more beautiful than the ocean,
because peopled.

And because you, mother, and you, father,
are not to be lived with
but only wept for in the night,
at Christmas, in the depths of winter.

Brabant is ever Brabant.
My weeping smudges the ink.
This gnawing which never stops
is at the root of my art.

I lie rocking
in my boat, the golden cradle
of an ideal existence
that can never be.

THE PLEA

'So I am cracked, they tell me.
Nothing, anyway, is going to change now.
Let me be broken open,
soon – in a summer garden,
or on the threshold of a crude hut.
Lord, kill me!
I want this plea to rise,
straight as an iris,
blue as that heaven.
A homeless fire, I roam out,
like you, and like you –

on our faces the same stamp
of strangers lost on the earth.'

MEDICAL SUN

This god is a medicine –
nothing weak or melancholy.

You can either worship what you see
in the form of a disc
or you can paint a mulberry tree
whirling the yellow
of an October sun,
shaking skin in a wind as it sheds blood

dancing.

The sun has never penetrated the North.

Here, it's as different as Morocco.
You are washed clear, washed clean,
and yes, land on another shore

strolling and at ease.

In the full tide of this flood,
under the blue sky, the orange, yellow

and red flowers splashed on the air
create a colour-wave, a soul-sway.
Giddily, you dive in.

You can't help but feast and rejoice.
Something is happier, lovelier,
a vibration, what is it? Happiness?

Even so, when you paint yourself
with wet ashes
into passageways,
watched by attendants, orderlies

looking for what was lost,
or perhaps never given –

then you are mistaken for something else.
And in the field below
the iron bars of this cell –

a reaper.
Who with his steady stroke
cuts away at the misfortune.

But can the sun sing by itself?

CONVALESCENCE

If they ask, say I have been too ill to write
and cannot move from this room
without risking a panic

and that my sickness is all earned
by the dumb fury of work,
under which I broke
and by which I was humbled.

And now perhaps there's a hole,
and because of this my strength leaks,
otherwise why am I here
in this hospice of forced rest,
torn half to pieces by the search for love.

Love's a bacillus, as they say,
and if that's so, then let me be innoculated.
The doctor jokes
that all painters are mad

and now here I am, this is my address.

On the other hand, you'll have heard said
that my attacks are seizures, I am not a loony.

If you asked a reason,
I would simply answer that there was no love,
I saw only stone
I began to petrify
and for that reason shrieked

against walls, against doors –
and yet remember no frenzy.

It must be true. Tell them it is a fact
what to me is rumour, emptiness.

And my torment is the not-knowing.
With my defeat and truth lumped in the one body
I endure the shame and waste.

But I have felt some calm visit me,
walking in the garden
where the poor fellows are.
It has a pond,
a shaggy carpet of flowers,
even an arcaded gallery that's whitewashed.
And how sweet and cool, how green, how many leaves!

But if I see the three black tree trunks
living snakily like serpents,
then I have to say
that what I lack is courage,
that it often fails me. And so
remorse sets in. Then I am
maimed, guilty.

Even without love I have turned to nature,
to the soil, and so grown from loss.
If this demon leaves me I'll grow again –

from a star
a rose
a cruel madness even.

I stand clasping nothing,
I am by a fountain
that is trickling gently with its cool silk
and hoisting gravely its wet flag.

I have told you, brother, what it is like for me.
This is my report – these empty hands.

from NOTES OVER A CHASM (1992)

TROUBLES

The train floods in. Under
the very bridge I am hurrying over.
It halts there. In the
sudden crush
I can't see you on the platform.
Until you stand before me:
cool, slim, mass of dark hair,
your small searching face.
Smiling your daughter-smile
that accepts much of me.
All that you have of me in you.

Hot streets beating with life.
I steer us through it
in the direction of the river,
a long dogged walk in noon sun.
We find shade near where the water flows.
You talk flowingly.
My head bends to listen
as our troubles, yours and mine,
mingle together in one single stream.

WATCHER

Nerve-cells are said to join
at a place called the synapse.
Or they have not properly fused;
do not precisely join up.

Energy pouring out
is sucked back as sadness.
A bacillus borne on the air.
And then the frightful anguish
of a loss.

Storms of cells. Wild fits.
Swarming fears, that the swifts imitate
at evening, skimming the river's skin.
Tiny insect-catchers, acrobats,
they fuse on an eye
focussed on nothingness, on
the flashing white of their winged breasts.

Steering by mere twitches,
angling forked tails,
arrow-heads in hurtling flight
with their synaptic tumbling,
their faint twittering.
And that ecstasy.

The lone watcher on the bench,
pierced by the miracle
of their ensemble flying
cries out his helplessness,
convulsed by the spasm of himself.

BACK

What use am I now?
Powers I thought I had
have fallen from me. Fallen back.
The tremor in my hands
warns me to wait. To lie still.

You go off to a tea party,
in an orchard, under boughs.
Flowering in your summer dress,
your white wave is anxious.

I stand like a tree, a post,
wanting to be forgotten,
desperate to be found.

VISTATION

Over its shoulder, shuddering,
I saw the birds, sunlight and grasses,
the whole earth that had moved off.

Dangling there, rocket-man,
how could I speak?
On your face the blank look
of someone registering a death.

Then it came back, ordinary and precious,
and all complete, so humble.
to the tiniest detail. Joys of the void.
And with your eyes, your arms.
Even the strange embrace,
as wonderful as the other was terrible.

PRAYER

The burnt grass,
the cracked gasping soil,
the leaves hanging limp
under blasts of sun
in the dead waterless air —

let it change soon.
Let the desert I have become
overflow with fountains.
To save us both from this drought.

Moisture in the throat,
behind the eyes,
wetting our parched lips.
Give me, Lord, a live voice.
the glory feeling, downpour of rose.

MOON

I consecrate this moment, this,
not ill and not fully well,
balanced over a pit
and all around
this garden of delights.

No longer damned,
for after all
nothing has been lost,
shelved maybe, then regained,
I wait here
stubbornly alive
in this precarious place.

Driving home in daylight
between the fields,
there was the moon, shimmering, regal
in its blue sea. Sliced
clean in half.

What is slicing me?
Only the littleness,
the wretched poverty of our imaginings.
A clean, empty moon,
I'll float back upwards into grace.
Effortlessly. In huge light.

HAPPINESS

Shakily, they stand up,
in the dark wood spilling suddenly with light.
Lonely spirits, their crushed hopes revive.
By his rising she accomplishes hers.

The sun's indifference has a grand majesty.
Ugly faces fill him with tenderness,
the beautiful are no longer cruel.

Grateful to be just here,
if he could only thank someone. Who, though?
They go by rapidly. The world of menace,
streets, it is now all good.
Everything speaks!

When he smiles, it smiles back.
Extraordinary, he can feel his heart
beating with joy under his shirt.

Then it is all too much. And he begins
to laugh. The clock's clumsy ticking
is a solace. Its oval face shines out.

Almost he can believe
that only he
understands what happiness is.

INITIATION

How to say it simply.
After a convulsive sixty years,
she rescued me.
Astonished, I was initiated into
the delights of heaven,
an utterly strange place
I remembered dimly from early childhood
as a sort of earth.
I would describe her as a naturalist.
Yes, she rescued me.
And I her. It was mutual aid.
We were delivered from ourselves,
the sun's jubilance welding us.

from FIRES IN OCTOBER (1994)

A TOLSTOY ROMANCE

The young man facing the light
can still be seen, he's still there
in the quiet corner where he often sits,
crouched by the hearth on a woven stool.
His age is thirty-two. It could be December.

It's a raw day. Because of this
he has lit the fire. Now the tiny
room of his cottage is cheery.
The flu he has still lingers,
so that he feels frail. It's pleasurable.

So is being off work. The other clerks
will be there now, in a city office
worlds away from this sea village.
It's like sitting at home, snug
and safe, when he was sick as a boy.

Childhood, Boyhood and Youth is the
book he's reading, by Tolstoy.
In the blue covers of an Oxford Classic,
with thin paper. It's a pocket edition.
Snow falling now all over Russia.

His little girl has gone to school,
taken by her mother, now back in bed.
Mornings, she says, make her unhappy.
Springs creak over the young man's head.
The tin clock. And in the grate, coal shifts.

On the lumpy wall a framed Gauguin print
shows a piebald dog, curled near the
foot of a Tahitian woman. Room in a trance,
like his. Through its open door
you go on a journey up a road.

He goes back to childhood on it.
And on those sparkling words, reading
them in ignorance as a true record.
Fooled though he is, somehow he knows.
He is suddenly thrilled by his own life.

105

How can he, a nobody, sit here
in concord and feel the equal
of someone so great? He does, though.
Maybe the words used by greatness
are always simple and humbling like this.

Crouching, his knees touch. He makes a vow.
One day he will have words flow
and ring as truly, in as cold a world.
He has tried already, but it isn't right.
The bit of fire sinks down. The sad mother calls.

ALONE

I look by chance out of the kitchen window
and there it sits – no, squats, soft-balled paws
and sheathed claws tucked out of sight, under the
forsythia on the grass cut only yesterday.
It's grey and white, a young thing.
It stares back, straight at my face
as if asking, 'What are you going to do?'
How neat! What a nice surprise!
Squatting there all compact, like something
carved in softest fur.

                              I can't see any birds.
When I open the door and make reassuring noises
it keeps staring. Fear in its eyes.
Then it runs off.
That shouldn't matter. Such a pretty sight,
and just passing through.
Not a sad stray like that other one.
I wouldn't have wanted the responsibility of it.
It's a lone animal that comes and goes.
And so unflatteringly occupied
with its own business.

STINGERS

Leaning on the stone parapet I see
them below me, near the stile:
a bed of nettles, with those green cushions
touching, lolling together. Plump, juicy.
Stingers, we called them when we were boys,
and went yelping off to bandage wounds
with cool fleshy docks.
                                    What I can't
get over is how soft they look!
Such opulence. And, if you like, deceit.
I have to admire those soft shapes
just asking to be rolled in.
With their thousand fangs, their
near invisible poisoned hairs.

Careful, I warn – as if my body's
naked. It has taken a long time
in this life to develop wariness
against traps, snares, delusions.

MORE LIGHT

You would turn this house into a little Italy
if you could, a place of secrets, shadows,
candlelight, shutters. We are both secretive
but in different ways. Windows behind veils –
nothing is too private for you.
I call for light everywhere: light in the kitchen,
in the recesses of my being, in my black corners.
You want the world shut out,
yet in your letters, see – the door
of your heart flies open.
Here on the ground, a crawler, I crave flight,
to be the opposite of what I am.
But what you want, you are. On tarmac, taking off,
you exult with the plane
in the shining leap of its escape.

There's an ancient Chinese curse:
'May you have an interesting life!'
Now that I'm loved, now I return the gift of love,
the curse is lifted and I can want the substance
of things. Redcurrant bushes that drip blood,
feasts of fruit, days following days,
darkness becoming light. You are capacious, dark.
Your smile glimmers. You give off that smoky light
of yourself. It gets late, and I'm not ready
for death. Only because of you, dark one,
is this house a home. A blood-luminous place.

BORDER COUNTRY

Late October. The sun honeyed,
warm as a summer day. Short of food,
we drive over the border
towards the market town.

A man in his fifties, on
a bend, heads for us
on the country road. Naked to the waist.
Wild-haired. Shambling and fast
in a way that looks eccentric somehow.
We pass by. We can see his flab.

In the old days there would
have been some sign, an exchange of
greetings maybe. The man stares,
unsmiling, fierce.
Why should it mean anything?
A man on a road in late autumn
who feels the heat. Likes it.

We are deep in peaceful fields,
light falling
over the strange nakedness
of things on earth.

SALVAGE

He was my uncle. Then he died.
The year before, friends arranged
a reunion for us – after fifty years.
I shake the hand
of a small man sceptically grinning,
and he leads me in.
He's alone now. His sons visit.
I search in his face, seeing the other's ghost.
Or think I do.
But he isn't baffled, like me.
No, he is back there, swept by his flood.
I take care not to impede it. Not that
anyone could.

        The other Harry was quiet.
Tubercular, even then, jerking his hand
with a sharp gesture when he had to cough.
Fastidious, handsomely ill, gaunt cheekbones
and a subtle smile
sneaking under his nose.
Silent as his wife, who, it is said,
died of an overdose. No one seemed sure.
But she was dead.
Of melancholy, I always thought.

Harry's mandolin hung on the wall.
I remember it from those days.
His delicate picking, in the brick house
among grassy ground on the edge
of town. Dorothy would bring
his tea. Only a boy,
I loved the shadows of this mournful couple.

Now he talks on, unstoppable,
his death close. Before I leave
he plays something, by request.
Uncertainly. The notes weak.
Only his memory is strong, strong.

CLEANING THE OVEN

It can't be bad, you think,
or it can wait a while. With a hidden
place you can at least pretend.
One day, sleeves rolled, you are
feeling righteous, and you attack the filth.
Strip the lining, have the disgusting truth
out on the kitchen floor
in broad daylight, where it can be seen.
Then set to work.

Oven pads, hot water, rags, and
in an hour you're getting somewhere,
so you think. But nothing will rid you
of these indelible stains. They cling on.
Old as insults. They've been there too long.
And then you say it. Reminders, they are.

Things begin to look better, there is less
disgrace, but you have to say that
the glory you hoped for isn't going to shine.
The dark that sticks there seems to belong.
Another world exists, with other rules,
behind that door.

I lived alone once for a time. Loveless.
A kind friend came to me with love.
Full of simple goodness, falling
on her knees and slaving half the day
on my cooker, that I thought was clean.
Until it shone like an altar of white bone.
When I thought she'd done she started again.

Then a kind of rage drove me to saying:
Leave it, enough's enough for God's sake!
Get right away from the damn shining thing!
I'm not an angel, and there's only me
living day by day like an animal here.
And anyway, nothing is going to change.

110

BIRTHDAY NOTES

The dogwood's leaves missing.
Ripped off in last Tuesday's gale.

The Jehovah's Witness, after knocking
this door for weeks, caught me.
A small, bouncy man. Wife in his car.
I paid for a leaflet on hellfire.

Go with my wife in rain
to look at hatchbacks. She might
lease a Nova. Has it got F.M.?
Can it play cassettes? And as an afterthought,
how many miles to the gallon?

Mugginess, cloud-cover. How my friend
would have hated the loss of light.
Out of agony now, in his total dark.

I can hear the tuner next door
at the disconsolate widow's piano.

Today's my sixty-fifth birthday. 'You were
never lovelier,' says the card, in print,
from my step-daughter who forgot to look.

Flowers all bedraggled. Birds sparse.
Nothing stirs in this blanket wet.

The gift weighing heavy. Knobbly and compact
as a grenade. Explodes peacefully,
half the size of my hand, the black casting
of an Indian head. Female. From you.

THE CURVE

How could I have missed it?
The path swinging over the recreation field,
flanked by high trees,
is a long beautiful curve.
Sweeping in one direction towards the village,
it takes us the other way
as gracefully,
swerving back into the land of forefathers.
Farm country, wheatfields.
Cows and a bull.
In the far distance a bank of hills.
Pliant willows edging to water
as we follow the river downstream,
winding into its curves.

It's the curve that's everywhere in life.
Deep in my own concerns
for two years or more,
unbelievably I missed seeing it.
I lift with it now. When you no longer do,
is it the slippery fall down out of life?
When the arc you don't see
takes you down, not up.
You don't see it because it's you.
Then the last trace,
that's fading on the day
the curve dies, crests over, and starts
reversing into fall.

PHOTOGRAPH OF MY INFANT CLASS

Broad river of autumn. Old man's beard.
On a dank morning, two days to go
before my pension I sit studying this scene.
It floods in over half the classroom
on a bright special day,
that immemorial light spoken of by poets,
'ancient beyond memory or record'
as my dictionary says.

All I can think is: gone.
Before a glass-fronted bookcase
is the propped notice inscribed in white:
All Saints Infants 1. That's us.

The source of light missing. Off
to the left by the brick windowsills
and the small jamjars of flowers.
'Second row on the right,' says the
photo's blank side in my mother's loose hand.

And there I am. Dressed like Ken Abel
in his wool jersey and string tie
with horizontal stripes. Under
the shiny tables those flat tins and boxes
where we stored belongings.
Mine said *Woodbines* in green letters.
Grains of tobacco still visible, fragrant.

That must be Harbourne, surely,
gripping his tiny hands. Staring.
Well-fed. The wealthy butcher's son.
Or is it Eric, a playmate from Harper Road?
One of the girls in front
is that Dorothy Petch, bone-poor,
who stank as she sat. Like Bloxham, Jack.

All of us caught up as one
in this grave moment of '29.
Paradise it was, soon to be lost
in the stone prison-house of big school.
Wanting Miss Allen's love, her warm
story books, Christmas concerts, carols.
All things bright and beautiful, we sang.

We danced round a maypole once.
Rainy days were good, the wooden slide came out.
Only one thing I can't account for now.
In that safe haven of unplastered walls,
a stuffed animal, the clay pots on saucers,
pictures through glass winking in the light,
I can't see a smile. Our infant faces
in meek rows are wiped clean
as slates. Smiles gone
where all the voices went. The songs too.

113

FRUIT

Not wishing to witness the last rites
of her final departure
he walked into the fields of apple trees,
faster and faster as if pursued.
It was no good. What he was fleeing
clung to his heels like a barbed shadow
as he climbed the gate, hearing
a door slam, then the taxi start,
out in the lane.

And while suffering one death
he was drawing close to another,
the early death of an old friend.
Soon now the men driving in with trailers
would gather all these apples.
The wooden bins lay waiting in the hedges.
They fill canvas pails that hook open at the bottom.
The deep bins would rumble like stomachs.

Even then, at the last moment,
stumbling down aisles between laden boughs,
a sweet juice breaking in his chest
was flooding him with fresh acids
as it had filled the apples. Wanting him
to fruit. The misery feeding it.

DAD

He was irascible sometimes. Long-legged.
A tall, naive man. With his bony exposed wrists,
giraffe neck. Seizures of irritation
would break the calm of his last years.
City-quick, he was at times pig-ignorant.
From the industrial heartlands,
son of a servant girl.

His wife's questions would make him laugh.
Her helpless fears slowly wore him down.
Left alone, he might have travelled, risked more,
but she clung hard and then his boldness died.

After his death and hers I found it,
the pamphlet by Marie Stopes, upstairs
in the bottom drawer of the dresser, half-hidden.
And in a grubby envelope, a thin rubber ring.

Where the grief enters it is hard to know,
but I wish he had talked to me, *real* talk –
as you, Mother, did. But his kind were proud,
stiff-necked. He had large sheepish hands.

She went crying into every corner
till she could be where he was.
In a late snap they sit cuddling on a beach
like two children holidaying.
What was sex to them, when in the end,
before death even, they were as one?
When their tired flesh had been so long together,
and known so much?

ROAD

Loneliness and solitude
are two separate issues. Hope's another.
You walk from the first
if you are lucky. Though
it can't really be done. The human
season is a lonely one. Let's say
you try to cultivate forgetting.

Sometimes a place, a cottage,
can mean both. Or all three. To find
it suddenly vacated to a huge wash
of time by someone leaving in a hurry,
hatefully, can be the loneliest thing.
It may be all you prayed and hoped for,
yet it condemns you
to that dread tick of minutes
and the lonely ache of yourself,
the four walls that once sheltered
no better than the pillow you howl into.

Solitude can mean setting out
down the road on errands
to the market town two miles away,
on foot: you have never learned to drive.
Or simply to eat somewhere,
lonely maybe at first
and then surprised by weather, skies,
rustling in verges, even the
vicious car cutting out too fast to overtake
as it rips past you from behind.
Hurling a curse at it, reaching
the rough track that dips down
the other side of the hedge
for a few hundred yards.

And then halted by it all.
Wanting to stand there, mute, passed by.
So much confusion, loss, panic.
An old post rotting in a ditch
with its hammered nails and red wire
gladdening the eye for no reason.
The road above gone quiet.

OCTOBER RIVER

Seven miles from here, the same river
had held me as a boy. My father fished it
while I watched. Once he fixed another line
for me, baited it, then left me to try my luck.
In no time I'd hooked something and it was heavy,
dragging down like a doom. When I cried out
he came running, an excited boy himself,
shouting me to take it easy: 'Don't snatch!'
It was a two-foot eel, tangling my line in slime,
writhing on the grass, a horrible underworld truth
bulging with muddy force
there at my feet. My dad knelt to it, one hand
grabbing its neck while it thrashed its length.
'What shall we do with it, eh son?' His eyes gleamed.
'Show it your mom?' Shaking my head I tried to laugh.
I knew then I feared life. Everything I was
shrank back.

Swimming in it was a new fearful thrill. On a hired float
that was half-waterlogged I paddled softly
upstream, nudging beds of rushes, settled on by insects
and heat, spellbound by the lapping of some unseen peace,
in a swelter of quiet. Now the great umbilical fastens me
to it. Now I walk most mornings by its wide slow water,
murkily alive and stirring, breathing out its faintly
rank smell, glossy in the brown autumn light like chestnuts.
Admiring narrow boats that glide past indifferent.
There was a man who waved. And now the anglers,
spaced out, sunk in their holes along the bank,
unwilling to speak, or perhaps drugged by something.
Turning back to the house to wait again
for a woman as dark and deep as this
with her desires, endlessly flowing. As I flow
gladly in her love. We swim out as one.

Under us the monster's silent. Under us our old mud.
The violent thrashings have gone quiet.
I love the coil of a river as it makes it way
in packed earth. Most of all I love
the mingling of waters that meet calmly
in a ripening light, deep down under fathoms of old river.
Something I never hoped to know.

THE AUTHOR SITS FOR HIS MOTHER
IN HIS THIRTY-SECOND YEAR

His head angled three-quarter face
for the sake of a profile,
a lip-swallowed, narrow-eyed
expression conveys resilience,
sceptical and clever. Vanity, they say,
is a male trait. The long jaw taut
over the scraggy neck, the spitting
image of his dad at that age. But
too vain for specs. Hair black and short,
exposing those large ears. And, again
doubled, a clerk's wormy pallor.
Over thin shoulders the skimpy
brown cord jacket of the artist-traitor
he now is. He sits tensely,

117

amused by his triumph, ignorant of
his fate. His first novel is just out.
A rainbow bends in his young blood.
Face out of focus, he strains forward
in the simple garden.
Starry, the bright Michaelmas daisies
halo his bony head.

ELEPHANT

Drawing is like meditating,
a painter said (probably Matisse).
And sometimes it can be true of poetry,
at the bedroom table in the alcove
on still mornings. The mind sober, if
not exactly awake. And sometimes
naming things is benediction enough.
Outside the window a few people arrive
by rote, beginning with the milk.
I peer downwards, and there's the van.
The sounds carry, but I usually look.
We seek human contact. We're all strangers here.

The wet garden path leads us
into a new day. Everywhere
is soaked with the night's profuse sweating.
An air frost. Have just checked
the oil level in my wife's dripping car.
She drives off. The rose bed against
the fence needs hoeing. Ivy, nettles and
the odd dandelion have sneaked in.
The Russian vine, ragged after storms,
hangs on to its tired leaves. Light
flashes. Exhilarated, I notice flower bulbs
in a brown paper bag. My leg bothers me,
and for some reason I recall Annie,
in the corner cottage that time in Somerset.
When I held fellowships she fed my cats.
Knocking her back door with keys. To thank
her. Never once let in.

'S'orl right,' she'd mumble, burly in
old clothes and boots, more or less a recluse.
Her soap operas real. The sound barrier too.
'It came down in that field, ask Stan.
A big bang, that's when it broke.'
Credulous, suspicious. With an old dog
for company, too weak to bark.
She said once she had seen an elephant
in the lane, but it was a wish she meant.

GARGNANO

A late charter to Milan flew us into night,
into the warm wet of young summer rain.
Eager to land, not easily affronted by weather.
A second baptism it was, the sky sobbing
to have us back. But it sprinkled
soulfully for two days. Till we stopped
seeing the funny side.

                    The third suspect day,
on the lake down to Gargnano, a mist
lifting off the water. The heat smote us.
Quaint to read of these boats
in the brochures described as steamers.
There was one, not ours,
broad in the beam, rising up three decks
and with great paddle wheels churning.
And the rushing hydrofoil, that
German tourists call a *flügelboote*.

We are not literary pilgrims
so I forget the name
of Lawrence's love-nest on Garda, 1912.
All I remember is Gargnano,
the youth and jollity of those letters,
and that garden they had –
peaches and ripe figs, bamboos.
For eighty lire a month. The living cheap as dirt.

We come here as lovers. We're both Midlanders.
Out of the cities, both of us.
We don't need reminding that we can't live here.
Seizing on odds and ends, century-enders,
a little every day, that's how our lives
take shape. We step down the plank.
Stroll for ourselves through this tiny place
which in *his* day had to be reached by boat.
No railway. At the back the steep rocky hills,
conquered finally by Mussolini's builders.
Now a big motor road buzzes angrily up there.

In the lovely square and along the quay
all is spellbound, and as it was.
A noon heat drives us into church.
Then in the afternoon we sit watching
old village women as they emerge to gossip.
A barber shop dark as a cave
is like these Italians, sunny outside,
shuttered within. We bake quietly
on a bench, sun-dried and ancient for
a few hours.
                    Till the boat calls.
And with beautiful and quiet ceremony
floats us homeward.

WHAT THE YOUNG WRITER HEARD
Rhys Davies was with D.H. Lawrence when
he fell ill in a Paris hotel in April, 1929

I can't bear them these Parisians
people packed like this are so vile
I just want to scuttle
like a rat before they tread on me
I don't want to be North again not ever
it's gone bad it's evil and anti-life
it can go to hell this place yes all of it
you ought to rest now I told him
and he groaned cursed and said no
he wouldn't he was sick of lying down
then in the night frightened
when I tried calling a doctor he swore no

120

get away from the phone
do as you're told damn you
stay in the room and sit quiet
here by the bed it helps
he didn't want his wife who was in London
queening it he said
she was out to finish him
calling her a bitch essential as his liver
and he said Davies I can't sit in the world
unless a woman's behind me
he was sick of illness
sick of eating Beemax
the world's a lovely place if one avoids man
he asked for water
and said get your notebook write this
I wrote Lady C and it was the epilogue
to my life's travels and that made it sad
and did I find it sad
and I said yes
yes I thought so he said
I'm knocked up I'm at the end of journeys
I wish there were miracles Davies

ON A BALCONY

Imagine this man
gripped by a desire
to sit on a balcony, his own balcony,
and feel a southern sun
falling on his head. His forearms.
The backs of his hands, now liver-spotted.
A northerner, he simply wants
to know what it is like, his chest
filling with sun.

He has imagined this dream
and now it's happening. For six days
the balcony is his. There's a lake view,
for which he has paid a supplement.
He throws open the shutters this first morning

and exclaims. Como ripples below,
out to the jagged far peaks
he thinks vaguely must be the Dolomites.

As if he cares. He stands there
gripping the rail, open to great light.
A sleepy woman emerges behind him.
She has heard his cry. Langorous, happy,
she listens to his astonishment.
Drowsily she is also staggered by the view,
the beauty. They have come over
in the dark by boat, on the black water,
baffled by lights, tired out.

This is a new day. Her arm around his
waist, her hand squeezes. He will tell her
another time what he has always known,
that it runs to waste, all of it,
if you are not loved.
He hugs his wife, smiling.
They congratulate each other tenderly
on their luck.

VAN GOGH

Dear Theo, I met a woman this winter.
One of those chance encounters I love.
Pregnant, sickly, walking the streets
to get food. Know what I mean? Back of
Ryn Station. I was all alone there.
In a dirty wine shop nearby I bought her
a glass. Explained things. My burnt hand,
and the cousin Kee I had been in love with.
She thought it craziness, but she listened.
Oh, I was glad of company that night!
We stayed on, snow coming down,
then I went with her to her room.
She scrubs, washes, cleans houses.
Another kid is with her mother. Christine,
I say, and she can't get over it.

No one calls her anything. Sien, maybe.
Her brother's a pimp. A lazy bastard
she calls him. So you can see the set-up.
Mother a poor drunk, too old now to earn money.
Anyway, we got in bed, in the bitter cold
of that room. She told me my nose was blue.

Let me make it short. My room's close
by. I took this woman for a model,
not the full rate, but I paid her rent.
Can you understand, she looked ill,
worn-out, and that attracted me. I can't
explain. If I want to help
then I have to do it right. She lives with me
now. It's serious. She's got stronger lately.
I made her eat as much nourishment
as I could afford, made her take baths,
and do nothing bad. She shares what I have.
In a few days she'll give birth. The crib's
waiting here. Yesterday I made drawings
of it, touched with some colour. You'll soon see.
Theo, I might marry the woman. I have
to know what you think. It won't cloud
the sky between you and me?

ON READING A CHEKHOV STORY

The road itself was a kind of happiness.
We smelled the life that touched us.
Walking nowhere in particular was so pleasant.
The sun high and warm,
a row of poles with their wires humming.
We could hear larks pouring song
even though invisibly, way above the fields.
A train near the skyline
crawled like a caterpillar.
The whole of nature dreamed gently,
dreaming us along with everything else.
All we needed were church bells,
I thought foolishly. Suddenly they rang out
on this calm Sunday morning,
loudly, joyfully.

Smiling in a strange way, you began to speak,
without life or hope
but by the tone of your voice
telling me and me only
that something special and important
was being said. And who knows,
I thought, perhaps the time
was not far off
when our lives would be as pleasant as this,
warmed through by the sun
and made airy by the singing of larks.

from NIGHTSHADE AND MORNING GLORY (1998)

ASHES AND STARS

You think it is you,
I think it's me.
Or it might be the death
lying between us
in the closed room
hidden deep inside you somewhere.

It is none of these things:
just stars, just ashes.
Out of nowhere
a tear falls,
out of nowhere
a rose of perfect peace descends.

We lose each other
and that's terrible.
Kneeling as though redundant
at the graveside
joins us again.
Love's body waits
among pebbles, parched flowers.

IN PRAISE OF NOTHING

Overjoyed by nothing, by
the absence first of all
of terror, then by
the mere existence of things
alive and as they are,
yes and by everything he had thought
his by right,
and so spurned,
restored now in its full regalia
of ordinariness
in the commonest of grey light,
he wanted to kneel,
to endow even the stones and twigs
with haloes,
but instead stared and stared,
his eye praising
what his cracked spirit
had somehow spun from itself.

TRANSFORMATIONS

Exasperated, stiff
with a winter that would thaw
rarely, my father's gaze was feared.
And his iron wrists, iron will.
A grey stalking being
who propped everything up:
roof, walls. When he arrived,
plates came on the table,
the hot food. Cutlery clattered
and fell silent. Head bent,
he chased gravy,
mopping it with his sponge of bread.
If he uttered groans it was
high up, hit by winds like an oak.
His mother died: he wept,
he lost all his leaves.
You saw the shame of his boy's gentleness
as his gaunt bones appeared.

ONE AND ONLY ROSE

Suddenly it comes to rest
in the bare yard,
a sky thing,
full of the curves of flight,
and waits there,
balanced on a barbed stem.

I fetch you out to this wonder.
It has not flown away. A great creamy
heart of joy
to one side of the dry square of grass
has opened secretly behind the tree.

It triumphs over us,
or in spite of us.
Exposed in our bad faith
we kneel down,
clearing the bindweed

from around its root
but really worshipping with clumsy hands
the triumph of moon married to sun
in a shower of night rain.

HOMAGE TO BLAKE

Children playing in the street
you called Heaven.
At the end, buried in
the gloom and squalor of two rooms
and a cupboard, smuts falling
on visions, you looked out
on the rubbish of the world
sunk between banks of mud.
Then leaving one room for another,
which was what death meant:
your wife gathering up raptures,
emanations, dreads, understanding
nothing, believing all.

END OF SUMMER

The sap loses faith, falls back.
It's all over
in the summer's heart.

The pale day's debility
lets fall a drop of rain.
In the far north
a first frost seasons everything
with a touch of salt.

Beyond the fences and chimney pots
two rusty tracks
aim for the hills.

Bored with itself, the garden
finds a cat.
She comes loitering down,
sharp in her black and white.

129

Oh, she has been before.
And look how sure she is
of her welcome!

As if there was nothing else
we stand here, quietly gazing:
three creatures in a ring
round a saucer of cream.

THE SAME SEA

Behind the lens
an invisible sea. And such
brightness, freshness!
Perhaps the kind of cold
you get in springtime on the sea wind.

The young father on the beach,
his thin hands, shoulders,
hair thick and glossily black,
holding his child tight
as if the spring itself sat on his lap.
A tiny life pure as an egg,
solemn as he is glad.

The man's girlish smile.
Behind them both rises
the harbour wall, all boulders.
There on the shingle lies
a woven bag, spilling its picnic.

On the snap's grubby white card
his dead mother
has inscribed the date.
Looking at it tells him only:
he has got here. Across forty years
of the same sea.

The cold sun lacquers the stones.
The tiny skull, the thin fuzz
of hair against the cheap sweater
would have smelled fragrant.
Like the sea.
His breast brightened with love.

STILL LIFE

As if deliberately composed.
the oak bureau on stilt legs
back in the alcove
bears an astonished fountain
of stiff pinks.

Though the blue vase
my daughter made
is a failure in her eyes,
I have brought it home.
Close by, a white pottery lamp
glazed in a factory
bulges and shines.

Between them now
walks a demure carved horse of wood,
head sweetly balanced, raising a foot.
A brown creature
smaller than my hand.

It stands there
on a scrap of pasture
in the mind's eye.
The corner's silence
steadily distils
its brown grace and its repose.

TOMMY TIMMS

Far off in a lost time,
stiff in his serge
and a white muffler,
dog-happy with his round eye
he waits there in the back yard –
always a Sunday morning –
and is let in.

Fresh from church,
Bible large in a clean fist
he sits obedient where he is put,
scrubbed bright,
the only noise his dumbstruck teeth
blaring white at us all.

Hands and face lit red,
black hair a block,
bolt upright like a god,
his huge blacked boots
in a shine like him.
Happiness is what he cries
all over
and is given tea
without having to say.

PHOTOGRAPH OF MY SLUM MOTHER

Peering from the sepia print,
she could be Peruvian:
black hair straight over the ears,
and the narrowed eyes, gaunt cheeks.

Sallow. Wearing a coarse apron.
The cotton frock's white collar
that seems to shine

and the wary smile of the poor
anywhere, somehow ripening
from within.

This one steadying her child
on a wooden horse on wheels,
its neck clutched tight.

In the cramped yard
along with everything else
hangs the galvanised tin bath.
Handle and rusted hook

and these lives, and these years,
buried in black shadow.
Speechless, they move up to me.

NEW POEMS

RETURN

I think again of times
O I think of times
unrecognisable now
but just an ache away

Soft and sure as an owl
through a curdle of cloud
the azure skies of eyes
landing twice and then gone

the air unruffled yet
the room quiet as a wood
a new place in the world
for you and me.

TOUCH

Fading now those seventies,
empty-hearted on long roads,
pity raging back as hate,
cries hitting walls,
your human touch too late.

Through all the deserts
of dead streets
in circles in the dark,
caught in the recurring dream
of love's spark.

Heart bursting
to say a name
on a station wide as life,
flowers budding in my hand
and then your flame.

EUCALYPTUS

It faints, it stands up,
it bends down
in a deep curve
over the little pond,
it waits trembling
like a heart
against the fence
of the rigid world.
It doesn't belong here
but it's here.
Freakish, it draws attention
to itself.
It wants stars,
it has leafy balconies.
In the blowing wind
it's a wounded fountain.
Nothing stops it growing.
The night settles around it
and we hear tree whispers.
So tall, it waves over to skylights
like a familiar.
The birds launch themselves
on their way to the moon.

OSCILLATION

After the abyss of huge hours,
to climb out and find grass.
What a discovery in spring light!

Underfoot,
the snowy faces of daisies
at their devotions.
The bells and pinnacles
of the risen man's
new heyday in the blood.
The peaceful blitzkrieg of
advancing growth.
The tender grasses
of Walt's green religion.

Storm clouds, and then the blue.
The green and the blue!

Never stopping to consider
the idiocy of his fall,
and between breaths
marvelling at his feet,
at the little miracle
of his singing strides.

OLD MAN'S PLEA

'Be content with what you have,'
says my old failing father-in-law,
urging me to live well. A fading leaf
of a man, once strong. Barely able to stand,
his eyes watery and near to tears,
dentures loose in his head.
Speechless, I want to gather up his bones,
hold him in my arms, kiss his old face
before he falls, while there is time.
Time, time! And then dreaming
of my dead father and mother,
turning up to see them suddenly
on a surprise visit. The door opening.
How nice, how happy they are to see me!
A voice in my ear asks bitterly,
'Why did it never happen?'

ARCADIA

Joyous, the young grasses
oblivious of the mower.
Bathed in a tender breeze
the spires of delphinium
sway their electric blue.
So many years now
from my tremulous daughter's
first smile,
so many roses aquiver
in her flesh,
so many garden delights!

RED ROSES

It's not enough to say
the work is the life
unless the work is love,
beating like a heart
among its coils and rubies.

And these red roses for you.

Cages fly open,
the man locked inside himself
walks free. The work must be love,
with arms reaching out.
Look at the sky, all love!
Opalescent clouds
lower full breasts
over whole landscapes,
and on the body of the earth
great rivers run.

FATHER POEM

'Good lad,' was all you said,
and 'Take it easy,' to slow down
my passionate digging.
Allotments witnessed
my only efforts to draw close.
On your high shoulder
as a child
at speedway meetings
was the easy part.
In the silence of plants
I find my father again.
Earth under the nails,
a twirl of beans
decorating a cane,
you wait there,
ghost in the ground.
Are you waiting for me?

CAULDRON

Tall, fountaining green,
the blood-drops of fuschias

dangling again. Birds
swarming to their table,

babies and mothers,
frogs in a dream of mud

and in the midst of
this cauldron of rebirth

the June mallow
relives its glory days,

pink and watery on its hundred stalks,
soft as an aquarelle.

PRAYER

That spirit brother of mine,
blossoming with laughter
from a green stem,
wounded like me by youth,
by the torrents of flowers
choking our veins,
books, music, art,
by the deafening silence
of stars and graves,
who died suddenly before our hearts opened,
forgive my fear.

BREATH OF LIFE

He is dead now,
and he was never more alive,
hopelessly in my life, dancing,
a grin of pain
fixed and held before him.

Beautiful as his hands his sorrow,
small of stature, big with grace,
dreading his loved and maimed father,
in thrall to his mad mother.

Dear friend, wanting
my release as I wanted his,
filling with laughter
the very cup of pity.

At seventeen and for years after
it was he, fleeing,
the boy angel in the wilderness
who wanted art to save him,
choking on his own mephitic vapours,

struggling to fill some instrument
with his breath of life,
voice of the dispossessed,
an Aeolian harp set quivering

for men bound to suffer,
for those blind with longing,
their faces naked as rivers,
for the chaste joy of their desiring.

HOLLYHOCKS

Can they reach higher?
Can we?
Out of nothing, from
the dry rubble
at the base of walls
they shoot for the stars,
spurning water,
astonishing the gardeners.
And what glories, with blooms
the colour of night, bruises,
the dainty cheeks of girls,
lemony powder-puffs
stirring on lances,
equally at home outside palaces
as cottages.
When they sway imperiously
I think of youth,
mornings of trembling
and enormous arrogance.

SOUTH

Going south, the hard fist
of the body opening,

a generous southern hand
reborn, that had died

in infancy
and now comes leafing

through the blood
to receive the sun.

Who would have suspected
this new world,

waiting intact to be coaxed forth,
beckoned by women,

by the perfumes of gardens,
babes ripening at the breast

sluggish with warmth
as they sink south,

all the treasures of soft fruit
just out of reach.

Succulent as an orange
the sun rises,

rays falling everywhere.
The heart is invited.

OTHER BOOKS FROM SHOESTRING PRESS

MORRIS PAPERS: Poems Arnold Rattenbury. Includes 5 colour illustrations of Morris's wallpaper designs. "The intellectual quality is apparent in his quirky wit and the skilful craftsmanship with which, for example, he uses rhyme, always its master, never its servant." *Poetry Nation Review.*

ISBN 1 899549 03 X   £4.95

INSIDE OUTSIDE: NEW AND SELECTED POEMS Barry Cole. "A fine poet … the real thing." *Stand.*

ISBN 1 899549 11 0   £6.95

COLLECTED POEMS Ian Fletcher. With Introduction by Peter Porter. Fletcher's work is that of "a virtuoso", as Porter remarks, a poet in love with "the voluptuousness of language" who is also a master technician.

ISBN 1 899549 22 6   £8.95

A COLD SPELL: Angela Leighton. The first full collection by a much admired poet.

ISBN: 1 899549 40 4   £6.95

BEYOND THE BITTER WIND Christopher Southgate. A substantial collection of new poems.

ISBN 1 899549 44 1   £8.00

Autumn 2000

STONELAND HARVEST: NEW AND SELECTED POEMS Dimitris Tsaloumas. This generous selection brings together poems from all periods of Tsaloumas's life and makes available for the first time to a UK readership the work of this major Greek-Australian poet.

ISBN 1 8995549 35 8   £8.00

ODES Andreas Kalvos. Translated into English by George Dandoulakis. The first English version of the work of a poet who is in some respects the equal of his contemporary, Greece's national poet, Solomos.

ISBN 1 899549 21 8   £9.95

LANDSCAPES FROM THE ORIGIN AND THE WANDERING OF YK Lydia Stephanou. Translated into English by Philip Ramp. This famous book-length poem by one of Greece's leading poets was first published in Greece in 1965. A second edition appeared in 1990.

ISBN 1 899549 20 X   £8.95

POEMS Manolis Anagnostakis. Translated into English by Philip Ramp. A wide-ranging selection from a poet who is generally regarded as one of Greece's most important living poets and who in 1985 won the Greek State Prize for Poetry.

ISBN 1 899549 19 6   £8.95

THE FREE BESIEGED AND OTHER POEMS Dionysios Solomos
In English versions. Edited by Peter Mackridge.

ISBN 1 899549 41 2   £8.00

SELECTED POEMS Tassos Denegris. Translated into English by Philip Ramp. A generous selection of the work of a Greek poet with an international reputation. Denegris's poetry has been translated into most major European languages and he has read across the world.

ISBN 1 899549 45 9   £6.95

THE FIRST DEATH Dimitris Lyacos. Translated into English by Shorsha Sullivan. With six masks by Friedrich Unegg. Praised by the Italian critic Bruno Rosada for "the casting of emotion into an analytical structure and its distillation into a means of communication", Lyacos's work has already made a significant impact across Europe, where it has been performed in a number of major cities.

ISBN 1 899549 42 0   £6.95

Shoestring Press also publishes Philip Callow's novel BLACK RAINBOW

ISBN 1 899549 33 1   £6.99

Books of related inerest from Trent Editions

Robert Bloomfield: *The Selected Poems of Robert Bloomfield*

Edited by John Goodridge and John Lucas, Intro. by John Lucas

Robert Bloomfield (1766–1823), was the most successful of the self-taught 'peasant poets' of the Romantic period, a prolific and popular writer whose first book *The Farmer's Boy* (1800), sold an unprecedented 26,000 copies in three years, and won the praise of Wordsworth, and John Clare, who called him the 'English Theocritus'. In the 20th century Edmund Blunden, among others, was a great admirer of Bloomfield. This edition includes a selection of Bloomfield's prose prefaces, as well as explanatory notes, a chronology of Bloomfield's life and a list of further reading.

Price: £7.99 ISBN 0 905 48894 6

William Barnes: *The Poems of William Barnes*

Edited, with a critical commentary, by Val Shepherd

William Barnes (1801–1886) is justly renowned for poems which, using their own Dorset dialect, speak out for the agricultural labouring families of the nineteenth-century Blackmoor Vale. Many of these expressions of village and private life appear in this Trent Edition but, in addition, a selection of the little known poems that Barnes wrote in Standard English is also included.

Price: £7.99 ISBN 0 905 48895 4

John Clare: *John Clare: the Living Year*

Edited, with an introduction and notes, by Tim Chilcott.

1841 was one of the most productive, varied, and imaginatively moving periods of John Clare's long poetic career. Against a background of asylum, escape home, and then forced removal to a second asylum, he wrote during this single year over 3,000 lines of original poetry and paraphrase, in addition to a substantial body of prose.

Price: £7.99 ISBN 0 905 488 55 5

from GREENWICH EXCHANGE

WILDERNESS: 36 POEMS 1972–93 Martin Seymour-Smith. Admired by other poets from Robert Graves to Ian Hamilton, Martin Seymour-Smith was a poet of unfailing craft who combined an astringent wit with a deep regard for the joys and pains of being alive.

ISBN 1 871551 08 0   £6.00

All these books may be ordered through Shoestring Press, 19 Devonshire Avenue, Beeston, Nottingham NG9 1BS. Tele/fax 0115 9251827.